T0129567

Feelings of a Poet!

Broken & Left to Stand

Sarah Taylor

authorHOUSE®

AuthorHouse™
1663 Liberty Drive
Bloomington, IN 47403
www.authorhouse.com
Phone: 833-262-8899

Published by AuthorHouse 08/11/2020

ISBN: 978-1-7283-6934-1 (sc)
ISBN: 978-1-7283-6936-5 (hc)
ISBN: 978-1-7283-6935-8 (e)

Library of Congress Control Number: 2020914492

Print information available on the last page.

This book is printed on acid-free paper.

Introduction

I was born in St. Louis Mo. I was four pounds. I was born into a faith family. I mean God fearing God serving people and my grandmother loved God with everything in her. On 1983, the doctor told my mother that they didn't expect me to live long due to my small birth weight and the fact that my lungs had not completely developed. imagine the sadness and desperation that filled the room and everyone's heart. My grandmother had a Friend who was an evangelist she came to the hospital to pray for me. My mother said that she prayed and prayed for me. She also prophesied to my mother about me. She told her that God had said that I would live a long and healthy life and that there was a calling on my life. She told her that God was going to use me. My family was extremely happy to hear this! As God had declared I did live a health life and so far it has been a long journey with a lot of ruff roads, many lessons and uncountable blessings.

Chapter 1

As a young child we lived in Mississippi, with my grandmother, grandfather, mother, aunt's and a slew of cousins. Those were some of the best days of my life. Lots of love, laughter, fun, excitement, family and blessed days. I remember my grandmother used to pray for us all the time. She would put blessed oil on our forehand and in the palms of our hands. She would pray over us. I remember her talking to God as if he were her friend and she would always say Lord you said in your word that if we delight ourselves in you. You would give us the desires of our heart. She said I delight myself in you day and night and I thank you for allowing me to be able to do. As time passed my mother decided that it would be good idea to leave Mississippi and move back to Illinois. I remember the sadness that my heart felt leaving the place that we called home. We had lived in Illinois before and no good came of it. My mother had met my father who was a murderer in Illinois back in the day. She then gave birth to me and my 2 little brothers. At the age of 2 years old I somehow got boiling hot water poured, are knocked over on my foot. My mother went to jail for a little while behind this. During these many months we lived with my aunt who was self-centered. she did not have time for us. What little time we were in her care my brother was dropped on his head on the concrete as a baby. He began to have fluid on his brain so doctors had to put a shunt in his head to drain extra fluid from his brain down into his abdomen to lower the pressure and swelling in his brain. I also remember living in this house this 2story house where the windows were always full of flies and it was always a smell of death in the house. The land lord had told my mother to never open the door in the attic but when she did she found out that the people who lived there before us worshipped the devil and made human sacrifices in that house to Satan himself. While living in this house I made one of my little brother's drink some bleach my mother said that I was a devil child little did she know I was just a curious child. I was always curious about what something would do or how it could affect something. So as a little child memories and stories that I had or had been told about living in Illinois had been horrific and I hated to go back. Most of all I did not want to leave my family. It felt like I was in a world wind and my world was ending at this time I was no older than 9 years old. The day came we packed up everything and hit the road after six long hours of driving we were back in IL. My mother and stepfather myself and my 2 brothers and 2 little sisters. In the beginning it was ok we were still together as a family and my mother seemed to really care for us. The longer we stayed in Illinois things began to change. A year after living in Illinois, our lives altered so drastically. My mother began to drink heavily. My stepfather was a crack head he had been using drugs for years even in Mississippi but now he had become more addicted. I remember one incident when we lived in Mississippi. We were at a grocery store and my stepfather jumped on a lady back and grabbed her purse. As he rode her back pulling her down to the ground. he yelled let me ride that funky donkey while taking her purse and running and jumping into the car. He did this in front of us as my cousins and I sat looking at each in shock I could not believe it. He laughed about it and told us not to say anything to our mothers about it. He would steal things from the house and money from my mother and as time passed they started to fight daily about it. he would leave for days and my mother would send are take us to the crack house to look for him. My stepfather was an auto mechanic he worked on everybody's car in the neighborhood. That was his hustle and an easy way to get money for drugs. Sometimes he would work on people cars for drugs that was one of the biggest reasons he and my mother would fight.

By this time my mother had begun to drink more and more the alcohol was beginning to consume her and she was always in the streets. When she was home she always had a strange man at the house. We had more uncles than I could count. It became my responsibility to take care of my brothers and sisters because I am the oldest of 7children I cooked their meals, I ironed their clothes, I got them ready for school and helped them with their homework. I loved them deeply. I felt sorry for all of us I gave them their baths and put them to bed at night all at the sweet age of 10years old. I was forced at a young age to learn the value of hard work and responsibility. As time went on the days and weeks became month and time passed by so fast. My mother gave birth to another child a baby girl and I gained a new child as well. I remember not long after my mother giving birth. she was back at it she continued to drink and run the streets. One night she told me she was going out and that I needed to stay up and watch the kids and to keep a close eye on the baby like usual after she left. I cleaned the house and fed my siblings. I helped the little kids get their baths and put them to bed then I changed the baby's diaper made her a warm bottle and fed her as she was eating she fell asleep. I kissed her little face while I patted her back. I put her in the crib and set back on the couch after a little while I fell asleep. I am not sure how much time had gone by. I remember I woke up to my mother dragging me off the couch and punching me upside the head and cursing and calling me everything but my name. I was so confused and scared I did not understand what had went wrong. Then she said you are laying here sleeping and my baby screaming crying at the top of her lungs. She said that she was crying so loud she could hear her outside of the front door. To make things worse instead of her using her door key to come inside the house she broke the glass out of the window on the front door then open the door and as she beat me all around the living room with whatever she could get her hands on she told me that I better clean up every piece of glass. As I received lashes all over my body. I could feel rage and anger building up inside of me. When she was done she picked up the baby and told me to get my lousy ass up and get her living room cleaned back up and all of the glass removed from the floor. While I cleaned I could barely see for the blood in my eye. When I finished I went into the bathroom and looked into the mirror I had a knot on the side of my forehead and blood slowly ran down my face. I had a cut on my arm and bruises all over. I stood there with tears streaming down my face deeply sadden. wondering how my mother could do such a thing to me. All my life I asked God why my mother hated me so much but my questions went unanswered. I took a towel and wet it with cold water and held it on my head. I went to bed and cried the night away. The next morning as we got ready for school my mother told me that if the teachers asked me about my head I better tell them that I got into a fight with a kid from school She said that if they called her she was going to do worse than that to me. When I made it to school sure enough my teacher asked what had happened to me and I told her exactly what my mom had told me to tell her and she didn't say anything else about it. These times we lived in no one really seemed to care enough to really find out what had happened. So it did not make since to try and explain so I lied as I was told. Our school day had come to an end and we were on our way home I dreaded going home because I never knew what to expect when we finally made it home. My mother was standing on the front porch awaiting our arrival. I was so scared and nervous when we walked onto the porch my mother said hello children how was your day? We all said good and went into the house she followed and said I am getting ready to leave. Yall need to do your homework and chores and she grabbed her jacket and went out of the door that had plastic taped to the window. We did as she had instructed when we finished we ran through the house playing and laughing. Hours later we heard the front door close my mother called for us she seemed to be happy.

When we walked into the room we saw that she had a strange man with her he was so big and black he stood about 6 feet tall and weighed about 290 pounds she told us his name was Tommy and that he was her friend. She said that she had known him for many years she also told my baby brother that this man was his father confused as we were. We did not say a word because we knew better. Since birth me and my 2 brothers were supposed to have had the same father and we all had the same last name. She had told us that he was dead. She told us that he died at 19 years old in a fire in his grandmother's basement a fire that he started trying to burn the body of his grandmother whom he had killed. After introducing us my mother told me to put some clothes on. I was going with her by this

5

time my stepfather walked in and she told him that she was leaving the kids with him. They argued as I got dressed and we soon left. I remember we went by my father's mother house for a little while. She was also a drunk we left there and they went to the store my mother bought more liquor and they continue to ride and drink as it became later and later all I wanted to do was go home I do not know why she had taken me with her any way. I was bored and tired of riding but they continue to drive as I set in the back seat of the car my mother put her head in Tommy's lap I thought she had fallen asleep but I could see her head moving up and down and I could tell that Tommy was enjoying what was going on. Afterwards we went to this house that I had never seen before. My mother told me to get out as we walked up this long flight of stairs. I remember thinking God where are we? We went inside of what I thought was a big house. I mean it was a big house but Tommy lived in the attic one bedroom and a little small room on the other side of a small wall that had a couch and a tiny TV. My mother put me on the couch and her and Tommy went into his room where they continue to drink and talk for what seemed like forever. Tommy called me into the room and said I know that you don't remember me but I remember when you were a little bitty girl. He said you used to look like a bunny rabbit. He told me that he loved my mother then and now and he asked is that OK with you? I just looked at him and before I could say anything my mother told me to go lay down and I went and laid back on the couch till I finally went to sleep. When I woke it was morning and I needed to use the bathroom really bad but there was no bathroom up there and I knew not to wake my mom I just laid there shaking and praying that I did not wet myself. About an hour later my mother finally got up I told her that I really needed to use the bathroom and she gave me a Cup that she had been drinking out of the night before and told me to pee in it. I did not want to pull my clothes down with Tommy right on the other side of the small wall. My mother said if you do not piss in the Cup you will just be wet. Tommy said that the bathroom was downstairs where an old lady lived and he couldn't take us into her house so I used the Cup. After finding out Tommy was renting this little room and did not have his own house let me know my mom did not need him around but who was I to say anything. We soon left and returned home where my mother and stepfather begin to argue and fight about her being gone all night. She did not care she said that she would do whatever she wanted to do then she put him out. Days went by and I was riding with my mother again she went down to a street and call it deuce 9. She picked up a strange man. I had never seen this man a day in my life he got into the car and he and my mom began to talk about him giving her money. He said that they were going to the hotel and she agreed. As I sat in the back seat I wondered what was going on and why she was doing this! she pulled up to the worst little motel and sent him in to get a room. When he went in she turned to me and said here take this gun all you have to do is squeeze the trigger. She told me that if she was not back in 20 minutes to come in and shoot him. She said I am not playing I mean it. He came back and told her the room number she turned and repeated it to me and then got out of the car. I was so scared I was freaking out my heart was in my shoes I did not want to do this. All I could think was I'm only 10 years old and my life is about to be over. I set there for what seemed like eternity looking around and looking at the clock on the dashboard 20 minutes came and went I sat there hesitant to move and at that moment she knocked on the window for me to unlock the door.

Peace fell all over me I was relieved and so happy. They got back into the car and my mother drove until she had returned to the deuce. Where she knew everybody. My father's mother lived on the deuce as well. My Aunt used to live on the deuce my mother lived there with her at the age of 15 and 16 the deuce is also where my mother met my dad so those where her stomping grounds for many years. She continued to hang out until dark and then we left and she took me to Virginia park. My mother always took me with her when she was doing stupid stuff exposing me to things that I had no business being exposed to she never just hung out with me or took me shopping are even took me to the park in the day time. She loved to go to the park at night we stayed for hours and after returning home Tommy met my mother at our house and he stayed the night. This went on for weeks my stepfather only came home from time to time at this point. My mom and Tommy just fell into a relationship a bad and toxic relationship. He started out acting nice but that did not last long. Months into their relationship he started beating her all the time I mean really beating her they argued every day. We had no peace in our home we never saw any friends or family and on the days that we were allowed to go to school we were made fun of because we were dirty. On the days that we didn't go to school it was because we stayed up all night taking turns rubbing my mothers and Tommy's feet are scratching their scalp or listening to music and entertaining them as if we were in the club. My mother would come home drunk and wake us up. She would say I want to kick it so y'all can get up and we would be up all night if we fell asleep mother and Tommy would beat us. My mother slapped me so hard one night my ears rang for an hour. For simply falling to asleep after being up all day running the house while she ran the streets and half the night and she wanted me to stay up and party with her. Hate being too fill my heart. One night my mother told me to rub her feet until she told me to stop about 3 hours into rubbing. She fell asleep and Tommy laid in bed next to her watching tv. Once she was good and sleep. He turned the tv to porn I turned away and he told me to look at the tv. When I refused he said in a low tone that if I didn't watch the tv he would tell my mother that I had turned it on porn and that he caught me watching it. I did not care what he told her! I told myself that my mother would never believe him over me. I continued to rub my mother's feet until I fell asleep at the foot of the bed. When I woke it was morning and my legs had gone to sleep from sitting on the stool so long my neck and back hurt from leaning over on the bed. That morning I told my mother what had happened. Tommy insisted that I was lying he told her that I was acting grow and watching porn and he had caught me and made me turn the channel. She believed him she believed every word that came from his mouth. I was infuriated in my head I wished death upon him. My mother called me a little hoe, slapped me and got in my face and said that's your problem you think you too grown and your nothing but a liar. That day my heart changed it became cold, and rage and anger engulfed my soul the woman that I had once believed in I did not believe in her anymore. She was supposed to be my protector but my whole life she had failed me.

Poem have you seen my childhood

Have you seen my childhood? Somehow it was thrown away lost and forgotten and stolen straight from underneath me! Have you seen my childhood? Where is my joy and peace my happiness and the people who are supposed to protect and love me when I am feeling beat down and weak! Have you seen my childhood? Why do I feel abandoned, and betrayed, neglected and enslaved? Have you seen my childhood? I have constantly been looking around. Shock has set in and still I have not found my innocence, compassion and peace and someone to love little ol me. It has been stripped from me. I have been robbed of my life and I'm left feeling broken and very empty.

Chapter 2

I talked to my grandmother today. she told me that she missed us she also said that she loved us more than anything in this world and that she prayed that everything was going well. I hung on to her every word and lied through my teeth to her because I knew that if I had uttered a word of what was going on in my mother's house are life I would have been found dead. She said I want to wish you all a happy Easter even though Easter was a week away. I hated to get off the phone with her she was my peace for a moment my happiness in the darkness, and she made me feel better even though I was sad. When the call was over I knew that I would go back to living in hell. My mother walked into the room and said ok you have talked long enough and took the phone. I was upset because I did not even get to say by are talk to any of the other family. My mother was always so mean to me. I am older now and I search myself looking for some kind words my mother had ever said to me and I can not find any. I search myself looking for life lessons that she may have instilled in me and I find none. My whole life the only thing that I ever learned from my mother was how not to ever be like be like her. That was not something that was taught to me by her but something that I taught myself from the age of 5. A week went by and today is Easter we begged my mother to go to church around the corner from our house. She and Tommy had been up all night long fighting and arguing about God knows what. They had been drinking for 48hours now the house was trashed from them throwing things, breaking mirrors and they had broken a window. My mother looked at me for a while and then she responded and said that she did not care if we went to the church or not. Me and my 2 little brothers put on our little rags that we had and walked around the corner to the church but when we got there it was so many people there that they would not let any more people in. We walked back around to the house and told my mother what had happened she became upset. She said that she was taking us back around there and she was going to make them let us in. What's so sad is my mother wasn't upset because she thought our feelings were hurt or we were sad because they wouldn't let us in. She was raging because she said that they are not that holly and she said that she would demand that they let us in are someone was going to get hurt. Tommy became very mad with her he didn't want her to leave the house. She told him to hell with him and left anyway as we walked down the street Tommy came running behind us he had put my mother's wicked jacket on she always carried 2 guns in her jacket pocket as he began to fight her we tried to help her and stop him but we were only kids it didn't move him at all. Tommy had knocked my mother down to the ground by this time my stepfather was coming around the corner. He saw what was going on and he ran to my mother and helped her up then said to Tommy you always want to fight a woman fight me man. I remember thinking Oh my God Donny is so little and Tommy so big. Donny squared up with him and Tommy reached into my mother's jacket pocket and pulled out a gun and shot Donny 2 times right in front of us and then ran off Donny laid there bleeding to death in the street trying to save my mother. My brother ran home and called 911 people started to come out of their houses to see what had happened. The ambulance finally came Donny was still alive but very weak from losing so much blood. My mother made us go home and she went to the hospital with Donny. Back at home we were so sad and mad all at the same time. We all hated Tommy and my 2 baby sisters wanted to kill him for what he had done to their father we didn't care that he was a drug addict he was a good person better than my mother and Tommy. Donny Still paid bills in my mom's house and helped out with stuff that we needed from time to time even though Tommy lived with my mother and he did nothing. when we would see Donny in the streets and ask him for money. He would give it to us and say don't tell your mother he had flaws but he cared for my mother. At 10:30 PM my mother came home from the hospital and told us that Donny was alive and that the bullet barely missed his heart she was very sad and she kept calling Tommy over and over. I finally heard her talking to him and she said I can't believe you shot my baby daddy and my best friend she told him that the police were looking for him. He tried to make it like all of this was her fault and he ran game on her talking about how much he loved her and that she needed to convince Donny not to press charges on him he told her to tell him to say that it was an accident after that she ended the call. I remember her playing Aaron Neville and Kenny G song even if my heart would break over and over all night long. We stayed up all night to try to console and support her as she sat and drank and cried her heart out for the first time I felt like my mother had feelings she actually cared about someone else other than her are Tommy. She seemed broken I remember her praying that was something she had not done in a very long time. She fell on her knees and she cried out to God she called out him and asked him to fix it and to change things. We cried with her and as the night came and went she became better and she went on to shower and get dressed to start the day. I want you all to know that in the mist of the storm God changes things it doesn't matter your situation it doesn't matter who you are it doesn't matter the circumstances you are still a child of God all you have to do is call on him and trust that he has fixed it and that things are turning around rise up and believe it and walk in it. This morning my mother got her things together and off to the hospital she went. When she left we laid down and slept most of the day later we got up and started our day same routine different day. We miss school today so when I got up I ironed my brothers and sisters clothes for school the next day, cooked dinner and fed my siblings, clean the house and put them back down to rest after many hours of them playing around the house. The day came and went at midnight my mother returned home and did the same thing as the night before. This went on for 3 weeks she barely slept and colt 45 and vodka was her and best friend. By this time she had convinced Donny to drop all charges against Tommy she told him to say that the shooting was an accident. She also told him that he could come home and that she would marry him and spend the rest of her life with him and she would never see are deal with Tommy again. I don't know what my mother had on Donny but she controlled him like a puppet. Donnie finally came home and we were so happy to see him we had not been to the hospital so it was good to see him still alive and breathing. He was really messed up though he could barely walk he had all of these bandages on his body that had to be changed and the wounds cleaned daily and he had a tube in his side. He also had all of these different kinds of medications he had to take throughout the day. My mother brought Donny home and put him on the living room couch he was not allowed in her bed. For about a month she took care of him. She really had slowed up on the drinking a little and was staying home a little bit more taking care of us. Finally she seemed to be getting herself together but after 2 weeks she started back seeing Tommy and being gone all day and night. As time passed Donny became stronger and in a few months he was back in the street's and back to using drugs and Tommy was back in our house and I lives. Donny expressed his hurt to my mother but it was made Clear that she didn't care. She was even bold enough to tell him that it was nothing he could do about it because he had already dropped the charges against Tommy. By this time things started to get very bad my mother continued to drink more and more she was always hanging out with one of her aunts daughter's our bills were not getting paid and she was pregnant again. Tommy was testing his limits to see what he could get away with he began to touch my small breasts are walk by me and touch me on my behind and say oh that was an accident. One day while putting his hand between my legs he whispered in my ear and said if you say anything to your mother she is never going to believe you. I will just say that you're lying. I was disgusted and so mad my lips trembled. Plus I believed him my mother always took everyone else's word over mine I hated my mother for this and I hated him. I began to contemplate death but I didn't want to leave my siblings I was their mother and protector. One night my mother left and went somewhere with some man and Tommy was in the streets doing whatever he wanted to do. me and my siblings were at home and me and my brothers were playing house I was the mom and my brother the dad we were clothes burning in our bed when Tommy walked in and caught us and he blew it way out of proportion. He asked where my mother was and we told him that she had left. He kept saying when your mother get home she's going to kill you. He was acting so I rate and hitting me upside my head. I told him that she left with a man. At this point I really did not care what happened. When he talked to her he lied and told her that he caught us having sex and my mother believed him she already had this foolishness in her head anyway and Tommy poured fuel on the fire. when she came home she and Tommy beat us until we could hardly breathe we tried to tell her what we were doing but she wasn't hearing it and she kept saying that I was a no good lousy hoe that was f****** my brother's and to keep Tommy from kicking my behind I told him where she was. She had caught me and my brothers naked together before but I wanted to see what they had and I was showing them what I had this was years before this and ever since then it was all bad. This lady was crazy I did not know where she was just that she left with a man. my mother was always accusing me of something even if it didn't happen and she tried to make me admit to having sex with my brothers, are me wanting to have sex with Tommy when I didn't agree or recall this happening she became very angry and began to slap me over and over and grab me by the hair and would tell me how no good I was. She did this often my neck would hurt so bad for days. A week before this situation my mother called me into the living room at about 3am when I came around the corner it was dark but candles were lit in the living room and I could see Tommy naked sitting on the couch with a woman on top of him. They were having sex my mother said to me that she was going to kill this hoe. I did not understand what was going on until Tommy started screaming and telling me to leave the room. I stood there in shock as he and my mother argued then I left the room. I could hear my mother saying that they were supposed to be having a three some but Tommy was more into this other woman. She said that they had picked the woman up off the streets because Tommy wanted her. Tommy was cursing her out telling her she was stupid. Then they began to fight. I ran into the room to try and stop them are to help my mother but the situation was beyond my control. The other woman was gone and Tommy soon left and my mother followed him. We did not see her again for two days when they left we had to deal with the cleanup used condoms, liquor bottles, and cigarette buts all over the place. These people where so pathetic to me. Had they not been doing the things in front of us and around us that they were doing we would not have been curious and doing the things that we were doing. My mother was always making up something in her mind trying to make me look bad because of the things that she was doing around me are to me are the things that she taught me. Like I remember one time we lived in Mississippi and I had a crush on my uncle and I just said that he was so fine. I was about six are seven years old I did not know any better. What I said was so innocent. My mother blew it out of proportion and told my aunt a whole lot of other foolishness that I was supposed to had said when it never even happened I was just a young girl with a crush that was it that was all but my mother had a cruel way of thinking and to try and explain it to others. They just didn't understand I was just a child so I was considered a liar automatically. A few weeks later we found out that my mother was pregnant again. She already had 6 kids I felt she did not need any more but I am not God. She was so mean (just hateful) and full of rage all the time. I remember one day she told me to make her something to eat I cooked her what she told me to cook exactly how she had showed me to cook it many times before. I took her the meal and she tasted it and threw it at me and told me that it was disgusting and that she did not want it she called me over to her bed put her hand around my neck and began to choke me she told me how stupid I was and how I was good for nothing. Before pushing me away from her she took one hand off my neck and slapped me so hard and with a grip still on my neck with the other hand she shoved me to the floor. She made me clean up every piece of food and that I did with no hesitation. I also remember she pulled a gun on my little brother and threatened to shoot him for God knows what. My mother hated me and my baby brother the most. She was just evil all the time for no reason and we were the ones that she took it out on. Due to the lack of money my mother and Tommy came up with this great idea that when we came home from school every day and we would go to scknucks grocery store and hustle which basically meant Panhandle till dark and then come home. So myself and my 2 little brothers would come home from school on the days we went and put our things down and go to the store from 3pm until 8.30pm taking people bags to their cars unloading their buggies and taking their buggies back into the store for a dollar or 2 maybe 3 are sometimes just change but it all added up and that was cool with my mom's and Tommy. We would come home and they would take every dime. they would go out and buy drinks and food and we would have to eat pork and beans out of the can. Sometimes cold and on a good day we would get some churches chicken with our can goods I remember Christmas was days away and it was sad because like every year before we had nothing my mother would say thank God that you're alive. This Christmas was different my mother signed us up at this church for a Christmas program and they asked us what we wanted and I remember asking for a CD player and Whitney Houston waiting to exhale CD and my brothers and sisters put in their request and in a few days before Christmas everything came. Christmas came and we were so happy but we were let down like always my mother took what she wanted and Tommy took what he wanted we were left with one thing I got to keep my CD player and a pair of socks my mother kept my CD and perfume we knew not to say anything if we didn't want to get hurt. The day after Christmas we were back to the hustle by this time my brothers had learned to steal very well. They stole food from the store, they stole money out of people cars and purses. They would say that I was the weak link because I was afraid to steal. We learned how to keep some of our money so the when we left home we could eat good too. This went on for six months then one day we came home and was told we had to come straight home tomorrow. That would be the day that my mother went to have an abortion. I was grateful and relieved. She was so ugly acting and an all-out bad mother, she did not need more kids. After she had the abortion it really did not change much. she was always angry because her and my aunt were supposed to have an abortion the same day and my aunt didn't go through with it and she did. She was five close to six months pregnant the baby was so big they had to send her home with rods in her cervix before they did the complete abortion and just like always she blamed someone else for her mishaps in life. After everything was taken care of we were back to the normal routine but instead of panhandling we now stood out on the street corners and in grocery stores sealing monitor newspapers for this lady who helped kids make extra money the papers cost 50 Cent and we made half of whatever we made that day we worked hard. On school days we work from 3 PM to 9 PM every day and on weekends we left home at 9

AM returned at 9 PM if we did not have $50 or $60 dollars each my mother was pissed. She would say you mean to tell me yall have been gone all day and this is all that you have? I remember one night I came home and I only had thirty dollars my mother slapped me so hard she busted my lip and I could hear out of my ear for a week she then told me that she was going to start making me stay home from now on. I knew that she was lying my mother never worked she received a welfare check every month and that was good enough for her. Tommy was a welder most of the time he didn't work and when he did every time he got paid he ran off with his paycheck and partied with his friends and other women. That is another reason why my mother and Tommy fought all the time. All of the money that came into the house my mother was drinking it up and Tommy was doing whatever he wanted to do with it. our lights were off for a month and when the lights were finally back on the gas was turned off. The stove was electric and since it was cold my mother turned the oven on and put a fan in front of it to circulate the heat and she pushed on. After selling newspapers for about 5 months my mother and Tommy got greedy my mother began to send Tommy and Donny to rob us and take all of the ladies money so if I sold 200 papers they took 100 dollars from me.

This happened to each of us twice and the lady fired us we lost our paper jobs over their foolishness and now had to be back at home every day all day with the drama and fighting. My mother started being missing in action for days and sometimes a week at a time and when she was home she was a drunken mess are sleep I don't know what my mother had on Donny but he was back in the picture and he was living with us again and as time went on he became just as screwed up as my mother and Tommy. There are now 3 grownups living in our household and we are getting ready to be evicted my mother found a hotel for us to live in for a while. I would never forget this was one of the worst little hotels there was and it smelled like old wet clothes. My mother put the kids in one room and the adults in the other. When morning came I remember hearing my mother screaming hysterically. Tommy and Donny had been gone all night together when they returned Donny was a bloody mess the story was Tommy and Donny went to get some drugs and Tommy let Donny out at the drug house while Donny was in the drug house he was almost beaten to death and to get away from the guys that were beating him he jumped out of a big picture window. He ran to the car that was down the street at the gas station with Tommy in it the guys chased him and Tommy allowed them to bust the window in the car drag Donny out of the car and continue to brutally beat him more and more. When they finished beating him Tommy picked him up and put him into the car and headed to the hotel. When they arrived Donny was half dead just lying there blood was coming from every part of his body he had broken ribs, black eyes, knocked out teeth, gashes on his face. He was really in a bad way as we stood there crying and watching the grownups argue back and forth about what had happened we realized exactly how bad our lives were spiraling out of control no hope, no guidance, no peace just chaos drama and bad days. Like before my mother left us and took Donny to the emergency room. He was in the hospital for an extended period of time and we stayed at that little ran down hotel until my mother got a voucher for the lady of snows. We stayed in a hotel until my mother got a place. By this time Donny was back on the streets and back to his same old tricks after he was released from the hospital my mother had completely lost her mind she was becoming more and more destructive in all of our lives my mother would always say things to me like you think you're so grown or I see the way you looking at Tommy like you want to eat him. She would say your nothing but a hoe and you are going to keep on and Tommy is going to stick something in you that you're not going like. I was so scared when she said things like this to me. she would always tell me you ain't shit and your life will never be shit. I could never understand what I had done to this woman for her to hate me as a child the way that she did. Time continued on and we moved from the hotel to a place which was also a part of Illinois. Life went downhill things became bad and out of hand

Poem

Broken hearts!

Where do broken hearts go when they feel like they no longer belong? When do you realize that love doesn't exist and the flame that once burned is truly gone? How much time do you put into something before you honestly understand that it is all a waste, and how do you heal the pain of knowing that time can't be given back or replace? Where do you get the strength to pull yourself up from such a low and how do you teach your heart to give up and simply just let go? They say that home is where the heart is but what if you lose your way and you've done all that you can do and prayed all the prayers that you know how to pray? Then you begin to feel like your life was curse the day that you were born and in all of the madness your soul was removed, and your heart completely torn.

Chapter 3

My mother gave birth to her seventh child today a baby girl she had a see c- section and the wound was not healing properly because she was fighting with Tommy day and night the hospital began to send a nurse out to the house to dress my mother's incision and to make sure she was on bed rest. I was the mother I took care of my mother and brothers and sisters. I hated it but I had no say in the matter. My mother finally healed and was back to her old ways she would leave home and be gone for 2 and 3 days and Tommy would come harassing me talking about where she was and that he knew I knew because she was always taken me with her when she was doing some bull crap. I told him that I didn't know where she was and he slapped me to the floor and grab me by the shirt and dragged me out of the house to go look for her with him or maybe he thought that I would take him to where she was. I knew of a few places that my mother could have been but I didn't tell him I was more afraid of my mother then I was of him I knew that she would kill me! I was forced to walk the streets for hours with him looking for her with a hatred in my heart that rocked me to my core and the sadness in my soul that made me feel like I didn't want to live anymore. As we walked Tommy was trying to make small talk with me he kept saying you know the only reason I treat you like I treat you is because of your mother right? He said you know she tell me to do those things to you. I never said a word in my mind I cursed the heavens I cursed the earth I cursed everything and everyone around me. He kept saying do you hear me talking to you I just kept walking and more anger filled my soul as the tears streamed down my face. Everything that he said to me entered my mind and became stuck in my throat and chest. Like a horse pill that I just could not swallow I hated him and my mother. We finally went back to the house and I put my little sister's to bed after feeding them then I went to bed as I laid there. I heard Tommy say that he was leaving. Donny was still there with us. In one room my mother had 2 sets of bunk beds 4 beds in all me and 3 of my little sisters shared a room but this night Donny slept in the room with us on the floor I laid in bed for hours looking at the ceiling until I finally fell asleep. I woke up in the middle of the night to Donny with his hand in my panties touching my vagina and he whispered in my ear and said this is our little secret don't tell anybody. I was so scared, and disgusted as I laid there and he penetrated me with his fingers and then put his finger in my mouth. As he took his fingers out of my mouth I just laid there with tears rolling down the side of my face. He left the room and I just laid there unable to move devastated, broken hearted, and overwhelmed while all these emotions flowed through me all at once. I had no one to tell I could not believe it. Donny was like a father to me I thought he had our best interest at heart and that he would protect us but at 11 years old I found out that I was living in hell and there was no God and all of the people that were in my life had failed me. I wanted to die, I wanted to kill everybody my heart was completely cold. I stayed awake the rest of the night and all day the next day trying to make sure he did not touch any of my sisters. My mother came home a day later. Tommy and her walked in together and they argued from the time she came in the door. Donny had the audacity to tell me that if Tommy put his hands on my mother I needed to jump out of the window and go call the police. I could not believe that he spoke to me like nothing had happened I was shocked. I just stood there dumbfounded Tommy walked out the door and I pulled my mother to the side and told her that Tommy has slapped me an dragged me out of the house to make me take him to where she was I told her that I didn't tell him anything. She was so angry she said little hoe you ain't shit and you will never be shit she said so now what I guess you and him are screwing huh? I said no mama and she said well why is he confiding in you then? I was shocked and at a loss for words I couldn't believe she was saying something like this to me again. I paused and then I told her that I had woke to Donny with his hands in my panties and he told me that it was our little secret and she turned and looked at me with a death look in her eyes and said trick let you tell it everybody wants to Fuck you. She told me to get my lousy ass out of her sight. The more I dealt with my mother the more empty I felt inside. I wanted to leave, but for my brothers and sisters I stayed around and pushed on. The thought of running away crossed my mind many times but I could not bring myself to just leave my babies. As I sat in my room She ate and went to bed. I did not know where Tommy was, but I was glad that he and Donny had left that night we prepared for the next day and went to bed. The next day we went to school when we came home. The house was locked up we knocked and knocked, and we knew that someone was home because my mother's car was in the driveway, but we got no answer.

We tried to go in through the window but for the first time, all of them were locked so we stood outside for two hours. Then Tommy came home talking stupid about us being outside. Then he saw that he could not get in either. She had barricaded the front and back doors so he broke the window and went in but he was locked in the room because she had wrapped pantyhose around the doorknobs pulled the door shut and tied the other end of the pantyhose to another door to keep the doors from being open. Tommy sent my brother next door to get a pair of scissors from the neighbors so he could cut the pantyhose off the doors. After he got the bedroom door opened, he opened the front door for us, and my mother laid there on the front room floor with blood all over her it was blood on the walls and floors glass was broken all over the room. My siblings and I cried in fear we kept calling her name. Tommy picked her up off the floor. She was breathing that was a relief. We could see that she had cut herself all over her own arms. That is where the blood came from. This was not the first time she had cut herself many times before. At first, we were sad and did not know what to do. We did not understand but the older we got we knew why she was doing it, and to me. I felt like it was sad, and pathetic. I used to think that one day she would die, and our lives would be much better. I told myself at 11½ years old. I would never be like her I had been telling myself this ever since I was 5 years old and I was constantly reminding myself of it. To me she was so weak and just unstable and the worst mother a child could have ever asked for. After this event She did not drink for a week and she stayed home in her room and in bed and me and my brothers catered to her and Tommy bringing them their meals and drinks or anything else they ask for or needed. I hated when they were home because we were always on foot and hair duty. I hated touching Tommy's feet and playing in my mother's hair was not any better. I was tired of staying up all night acting like their slave. After being up all night I still had to make sure the kids eat got baths and the house was clean and every time I turned around somebody was bringing home a stray dog at this time, we had four dogs more mess to clean up. During my mother's recovery time our house was peaceful, no arguing or fighting, no one being accused of anything and no one being sexually molested but we still walked around like we were on eggshells. This is the most peace that we had in our house in a long time, but it did not last long. Those seven days came and went fast and her and Tommy were back to the same old foolishness. Tommy was cheating with some chick and my mother had found out. They fought and broke the mirrors on the walls throwing things at each other. My mother stabbed Tommy and he punched her in the face and ran out of the door. My brother had jumped out of the window and went and called the police but when they came. My mother told them that everything was fine, and he was gone. We had called the police to our house over 100 times in the little time that we had lived there. They would lock Tommy up and my mother would bond him out, and when they locked them both up in a day or two, they both would be out. The cops and DCFS came to our house so much, it was like a joke when they came and sometimes, they did not come. We had no help the police looked at my mother like a fool. They would tell her if they had to come out again, they were going to take the kids and lock her and Tommy up, but they never did take the kids while I lived there. When Tommy ran out my mother sat on the floor crying like her world had ended. My brother hugged her, I just stood there looking at her. I could not understand how she loved this man more than her own children. I had never saw her cry over are for none of us our sadness did not make her sad, our hurt she could not feel. She sobbed for a while then she got up and cleaned herself up she told us she would be back and not to open the door for anyone. When she left, we did what we seemed to always be doing which was cleaning up after them. we threw away all the broken glass and waited for mother to return home. Even though my mother was a mess and full of hell we still loved her. We just hated the way she treated us. Days went by and she still had not come home. On the fourth day she came home. She had blood all over her and her car was gone. She and Tommy had been fighting and he made her crash her car into something. She had knocked out her front teeth and broke the rest of them off. She was so angry when she came into the house, she began to curse and scream at us, saying that Tommy said she needed to come home and feed her kids, she said Fuck these kids, what about my life. I tried to reassure her by telling her that everything was fine and that everyone had eaten, and we all had already taken our baths. She did not care what I was saying she just continued to rage. She said "that's the problem, you think you are so grown don't you ". Before I could say anything, she grabbed me and threw me against the wall and start to choke me. The grip of her hands around my neck became tighter and tighter. I began to stop breathing. I could see my siblings standing in the distance, terrified, crying, and unable to say a word as I gasp for air. The only thought in my mind was kill me, kill me, please. Then I could feel my body sliding down the wall. Everything became so peaceful. For the first time in my life. There was no pain, no hurt, and no sorrow no sadness. Then I saw this beautiful bright light, but it did not last long. I came to, and I was laying on the floor back in misery and she still was ranging. She grabbed me up and she said to me "since you think you are so grown, take off everything you have on." She said, "I paid for it". I stood there crying and begging her, please do not do this to me. I told her I would change, I would not be grown anymore, but still she insisted that I take off my clothes. She snatched every piece of clothing from my hands. There I stood in my tiny bra and little panties, crying my heart out. She said take that shit off too. I replied, "momma please, please". She grabbed me by my bra and ripped it off. She then grabbed my panties and snatched them off. I stood there naked and embarrassed in front of Tommy, Donny, and my brothers and sisters. I stood there and tried to cover myself with my hands, wondering what I had done for her to have so much hatred toward me. what did I do to deserve such awful treatment? Then she opened the front door and threw me outside. I hid myself behind a bush and cried. I did not know what else to do at that moment and talking to God was the last thing that crossed my mind. I would not have wished this kind of hurt on my worst enemy. I was outside for almost an hour that hour felt like a lifetime. I could hear Tommy and my mother arguing about what she had done but she just kept saying "you can go out there with your little girl friend". I looked up and saw my brother running from around the side of the house he had jumped out the window to bring me clothes to put on. He cried and said he was sorry that our mother had done that to me. He said sis, you have to leave! I do not want her to kill you. Then he hugged me and said he had to go because he did not want to get in any trouble. This brother was her favorite child he could do no wrong in her eyes. He turned around and went back around the house to go back into the window. It almost killed me thinking about leaving them.

I knew that my mother would start to treat them just as bad as she had treated me, but I knew bro was right. I pulled myself together and walked an hour to my grandmother's house, my dad's mother, which was not any better. She was an alcoholic as well and she did not really care about us because she hated my mother. I was 11years old, four days before I turned 12 and had nowhere to go. After I made it to my grandmother's house and told her what happened she called DCFS, but they did not do anything. my grandmother allowed me to live with her. living with her was not any better than living at home with my mother. My uncle and two of his friends would molest me. They would put things like pencils inside of my vagina and one day, they used a small flashlight. Somedays they would put their fingers inside me. Each time they put more fingers in. My vagina would hurt so bad I would just cry and wish for death. Sad part is it never came. they would also take turns making me suck their penises. They would hold me down and tell me that if I told anybody, they would do much worse. I finally got the nerve to tell my grandmother and she beat me on my lips with a ruler and told me that I was telling lies and I better not tell those lies to anyone else. I lived with her for a year. At this time, I was lost and broken. I could not understand how people would say God is real and so good and he sees everything. I guess he overlooked me are just did not care. One day one of my teachers told me that God had a plan for my life and my steps were ordered. I cursed her out and told her there was no God and she was stupid for believing that there was one. I was suspended from school for three days behind that, which did not make it any better. Every day that I was suspended, my grandmother woke me up every day by beating me with a phone card all over my body. She made me clean out the flooded basement from 7am until 8pm, with no food or water for a punishment. My grandmother was a toxic old woman and the whole neighborhood knew it. I really believed my life was cursed. I did not understand why I was so hated by so many. I was only a child and I did what I was told but that did not make any difference. No matter how good I was, the people in my life used and abused me. I was excited to go back to school when my suspension was over. School allowed me to get away from the things that was happening at home. One day I came home, and mother was sitting in my grandmother living room. I had not seen her in a whole year. I felt overwhelmed but I was happy to see her. She talked to me and told me that things had changed at home and her and Tommy were no longer together. She told me that she loved me and that she wanted me to come back.

Poem Hurt

Have you ever been hurt so bad that it shocks your soul, freezes your brain and leaves your heart with a hole? Have you ever had pain in your heart that was so bad it hurts to cry? And while you are trying to take a breath thinking it would be best just to lay here and die. Have you ever just been alone? Do you feel the pain of thinking that everyone is gone? Have you ever been so hurt that the tears start to come down? Your body starts to shake and then you hit the ground. It hurts so bad that you cannot stand to your feet and if you listen close enough, you will hear your heart skip a beat. As you open your mouth and gasp for some air your head begins to spin and you think to yourself that life just isn't fair. Then you come back to your senses and think, how could I have let life take me there? Where? To a place where love is no more, destruction and dysfunction seems to be the norm and the blood that flows through my veins have become cold, it is no longer warm. There is like and lust, material things a must and things like love and loyalty, trust, they put them away in a corner somewhere and they are just collecting dust.

Chapter 4

I hung on to her every word, wanting to believe her. Then she went on to tell me that she needed me to steal my grandmother's social security check. She told me that she did not have any money and my brothers and sisters were hungry and she needed to pay bills. I felt sorry for her and my siblings and foolishly I walked into my grandmother's room went into the drawer and stole my grandmother's money and gave it to my mother. My mother took the money and she took me to The Bazaar clothing store and bought me this little cheap tennis skirt outfit for my sixth-grade graduation and then took me back to my grandmother's house and left me there. I did not see her or hear from her for three days. She didn't even come to my sixth-grade graduation. My grandmother had found out that her money was gone, and she knew that I had taken it and given it to my mother. She beat me and cut off all of my hair and sent me to my graduation with the hooker outfit on because that's what it looked like a cheap hooker outfit nothing for a young girl and especially not for a sixth grade graduation. My grandmother took everything that I owned and burned it and then put me out of her house. She said let's see if your mammy come and get you. She called my mother and cursed her out about the money and told her that she had put me out. Hours later, my mother picked me up it was dark outside. On the way to her house she gave me this long talk about how she was not having any grown bullshit and that I was not going to mess up her life. I just sat there looking out of the window trying to figure out what she was talking about. When I went back to her house, nothing had changed things were still the same. She had lied to me! She made me steal from my grandmother for her and Tommy. They had moved into a duplex on a street, it was on the hoe stroll. The grown-ups stayed on one side and the children stayed on the other side. On the side that the children stayed on there was no running water, the toilet did not flush, and the smell was awful. She said that my siblings had broken the toilet and she was not getting it fixed. There were two bedrooms, the girls were in one and the boys in the other. In my brothers' room they slept on a mattress that was on the floor. The mattress was pissed out because they wet their beds. My sisters had a full-size bed and a twin-size bed in their room. My siblings were so happy to see me, and I was happy to see them. I had not seen them in a year. They began to tell me how bad things were and had been. They told me they barely got a chance to eat and when they did, my mother would only feed who she thought deserved to eat. One of my sisters told me that she had to regurgitate food to feed the other sisters. All this sad news saddened me down in the depths of my soul. They told me that my mom and Tommy had my brothers stealing and selling, drugs, as a hustle to take care of them. when I moved in, I realized that we stayed locked in on one side of the house, unless my mother called us to her side of the house are allowed us to go outside. Mother told me things had changed, but nothing changed. She still stayed up all night drinking and playing loud music. She even started to bring home multiple random men at one time. Tommy stayed out when he wanted to and started coming home less and less. Tommy and mother started smoking crack My mother though that I did not know but when I lived with my grandmother a few of the dope boys told me that they had sold her and Tommy Crack. My mother did not care about us or her own life. As the day went by, she feed us green beans and sent us to bed. I slept in the full-size bed with two of my sisters. The next day the lights were turned off. The lights stayed off for a week. I kept thinking; I had come back to the same mess I tried to get away from. We had to wash our clothes in the tub with buckets of water that we had to get from outside. My mother told us that we had to walk on the clothes to get them clean and we had to scrub them on a washboard after walking on them. Then we rung them out and hung them on the back porch to dry. When my siblings went to school, they said that they were made fun of because they smelled so bad. They smelled like urine, must and cigarette smoke. They said that they would come home sad and tell my mother about the things the teachers and kids had said about them and she would say "that's on y'all pissy ass. My mother never had anything positive to say and everything was always our fault. I just wished for once she would be a mother to us. One day my mother called us into her room and told us we needed to put on some decent clothes because our aunt was coming from Mississippi to visit us. I was stunned because no one ever came to visit us, especially not family from Mississippi. We went into our little Dungeons and put on what little rags we had. Hours later my aunt came she was not allowed in our house other than to use my mother's bathroom. we played outside and visited with them under a big tree in our front yard we knew better than to say anything about how we lived or how we were treated. We were just happy to finally see some family and to have a free day of fun and laughter with our kin folks. A while later the day came to an end and we hugged and kissed our cousins and aunt and said our goodbye's. It was back to the norm for us 3 nights later Tommy was home he and my mother were up all night, playing music and drinking they seem to be enjoying themselves. I fell asleep only to wake to my mother dragging me out of the bed by my shirt and hair. I was still half sleep and I did not know what was going on she pulled me over to her side of the house and close the door and then she pulled me into her bedroom. I could still hear the music playing and I could hear Tommy saying what are you doing? It was pitch black dark in her room because she always taped black trash bag up to her windows to keep out any light. As she held on to me, I kept saying mama what did I do but she did not say a word she began to rub something all over my mouth that smelled like Jelly. I was so confused I could hear Tommy talking but he was not moving around the room. She kept pulling me and at this point I could feel that I was close to her bed my legs touched the bed rail. I was thinking what the hell is she doing? Then she started to push my head down while holding onto my hair I could hear Tommy closer to me at first I didn't know what she was doing but I begin to feel tommy's penis hitting my face and mouth and I knew that she was trying to make me suck his penis. I became so enraged I started to fight her, and I bit her on the arm and she let go of me and Tommy laid there saying baby! Baby! What are you doing I think she had him tide to the bed all I could think while I ran away from her was they planned to rape me. My own mother was going to let me be raped by her baby daddy. I ran back to our side of the house and jumped out of the window because they kept the bars on the doors locked and I ran to the pay phone and called the police I waited outside on them when they arrived. I told them exactly what had happened and after that they knocked on the door and they repeated to my mother what I had said to them. she told them that I was a damn lie and that I was mad because she woke me up early to make me complete my unfinished chores. she told them that I was rebellious and that I ran away all the time and that I was always calling DCFS and the police. She said that I was always causing a problem in her house and that if they wanted to they could remove me from her house. I thought to myself this woman is crazy. I had not done anything and all the times I ran away and called DCFS are the police it was because we needed help. The officer turned and started talking to me he told me that I should be grateful to have a mother that cares for me. He said I needed to try to be obedient and listen to my mother and do as I was told. He said if I called them again, they were going to arrest me and then he told me to go back into the house. I could hear him and my mother talking on the porch and he told her that she should not have any more problems out of me. I hated the police and children and Family Services they didn't help the kids they were another let down when the police left Tommy whooped me it was so bad I could not sit down on my behind for days. My siblings cried for me they would always say Des we are sorry this happened to you they would hug and kiss me and tell me that they loved me even if our mother did not. I just kept thinking I wanted out of my mother's house things were going to too far. I also knew that I had nowhere to go my mother would always telling us don't nobody want yawl. She said the family knows yawl ain't shit and that they don't want yawl in their house causing a problem. My mother made us look like problem children to the family when we were just as bad as any other child. We did certain things like stealing food and money from my mother when we could because we had no choice but to do so. I remember one day my mother got her welfare check and stamps and me and my brother's stole all of it and hid it in the heat vent. When my mother turned the heat on money and stamps blew all through the house because the money had falling, down into the heating duct. We lied and said we didn't take it but she knew we had. We got in a lot of trouble but it didn't matter we got to eat that day. My mother collected most of the money and stamps but what she did not get we took it to school and bought food and snacks and treated the other kids. My mother use to say that she had the worst children in the world but what she didn't understand was she was making us that way we were a product of our environment and situation and we were becoming who she was making us. My mother told us no matter what happened to her we would have to go into the system. She would tell us no one is going to believe yawl. It seemed to be true the police and DCFS sure didn't. I was stuck and my mother made sure we all knew that. She always said don't nobody give a damn about yawl. She would say it is sad when your own mother doesn't even want you. 2 weeks later 3 of my grandmother's brothers from Illinois came to visit us we had never met them but they were really nice they caught up with my mom while talking about old times and drinking and playing old school music. We were allowed to come from our side of the house to visit with them for a little while One of my uncles gave me his number and said if we needed anything just call him I was so happy. I hid his number because I knew I would need it. Three days after my uncle left we were outside playing with Tommy's nieces we were on the front porch and one of them were playing with the lock on the bars on the front door and locked it. We continued to play for a little while then

Tommy came to the door and said Des. your mother want you. I walked onto the porch and looked at him and I said the bars are locked and he said go around back and come in through the basement. I knew something was not right I could feel it all over me. Plus I hated that basement it was wet and creepy and Donny lived down there he slept on a lawn chair with a tiny TV in the back room the basement had dirt floors and a musty order. As I stepped down off the porch I told my brothers if they heard me screaming to please come help me and they said ok. As I walked around the side of the house glass laid on the ground from mirrors that my mother had broken inside of the house and thrown outside. I picked up a narrow piece of glass and put it into my pocket. I told myself if anything happen I was going to stab Tommy and my mother. I went on into the basement door I was so scared walking up that long flight of steps. When I made it upstairs into my mother's room she was sitting on the side of the bed looking run over. Because she had been up drinking for 3 days straight. I said yes mama and she said in a very calm voice I want you to go into the kitchen and wash those dishes. I didn't want to especially sense we had not eaten anything in there but I knew what would happen if I refused. I said yes mama and walked out of her room through the other room and into the kitchen. I began to run my dish water when Tommy walked into the kitchen and came over to me and pressed the front of his body against mine and said since you are always acting like somebody wants Fuck you I'm going to give you what you want. I ran past him into the room right next to my mother's room and he grabbed me and slammed me onto the floor. I started screaming momma, mom's, help me help me please momma please help me. He began to choke me, as he choked me he ripped my shirt off. I kept screaming but my mother never came are said a word. By this time my brothers were beating on the door to my mother side of the house. I remember my mother finally came into the room and started fighting Tommy and he let me go and said what the hell are you doing he said you told me to do this. He started punching her in the face and he broke her nose. I jumped up and ran to the door. When I opened the door all of the kids were standing there. I ran past them into our room. I got my uncles number and I ran down the steps out of the door and to the pay phone. I called the police and my uncle he did not answer so I left a message and begged him to please come get me. The police came and arrested my mother and Tommy for domestic violence. I stood on the corner and watched the police take them away. I hoped that they would be in jail for a long time and that we would live somewhere else. Tommy nieces mother took us to her house. We were there the rest of day and most of the night her kids told her what had happened. She kept saying baby I'm sorry that y'all have to go through all of this. I just sat silently planning my get away. I could not take it anymore I needed out. My mother came to pick us up after she was released from jail. We went back to our house and she set us down and said that I was nothing but trouble and that I was going to get her and Tommy in a world of mess with my lies. She said that she had loved Tommy for 16 years and I was not going to mess that up. Then she said I had to go she said that she did not care where I went, as long as it wasn't in her house. I was completely lost I could not understand how she could choose a man over her child or allow everything that was going on and continue to call me a liar. I set there and I did not shed a tear all I could do was think how much I hated this lady. I wished she would die, and then I asked her where was I supposed to go? I asked her for my grandmother's number in

Mississippi and she said I do not care where you go. She said but it won't be with my mother or sisters she said you will not go and fill their heads with all of your bull crap and she said if you say another word I'm going to knock your teeth out. I was in disbelief I could not believe that I was getting ready to be 13 years old and homeless. Just so happened my uncle had received my message and came. When my uncle showed up my mother was putting what few things I had on the porch and I was standing there with my arms folded thinking I just don't give a damn. My uncle asked what was going on and my mother told him I had to go. He said go where and she said that she did not care. He began to take my things and put them into the trunk of his car when he finished. He said come on little girl and I went with him. He told my mother that he would be back for my school records. I was hurt only because my mother would not let me talk to my brothers and sisters and I did not get to say goodbye. I did not get to tell them that I loved them beyond measures and that I would be back to help them.

Poem moving on

Now at this point I am so far outside of myself or should I say beside myself, Fed up to the rim can't take no more. don't give a damn, have none that I adore. I understanding that there is no obstacle greater than thee not even family that works for me. No longer affected refuse to grieve trying to take a stronghold to keep from losing me. Looking for Salvation in this fucked up nation third generation trying to sustain myself from within. Trying not to let life or family become a burden. Determined to keep myself and my heart on a level most can't take, reminding myself that pain makes the heart toughen it came break. One individual that has so much to reveal and so equipped but still looking for a purpose just to live. Unlike most emotions are not my favorite thing, I can't relate to love and life it's too damn extreme. Disappointed and disheartened in the decisions that we all make. Overwhelmed and sick of wondering how much heartbreak can I take. Confused, misused and made an example of by a four letter word (love). Deprived the power to take possession of one situation that people speak so highly of and once again made a fool of by that letter word love. So now what do I do? Do I walk away? or should I say move on? That is what's best because my heart and soul feels like it's gone or maybe I should say no longer belong.

Chapter 5

My uncle took me to his place. He lived in a one bedroom apartment and he shared it with his little brother uncle C. When we arrived uncle C was laying on the couch with his head phones in his ears singing very loudly. When we walked in he started laughing and said what's up dirty! I said hi, uncle G took me into his bedroom. He began to set up a roll away bed that he pulled out of his closet after he finished. He pushed it into the corner beside his bed. He then sat me down and talked to me. He said I do not know what it is that you have been through in life I'm just here to make it better. He said I just need you to trust me we are here for you I set there scared out of my mind. I just knew that they were going to hurt me and cause me harm. I agreed to stay anyway. My uncle G asked if I was hungry? I said yes and at 3 AM he took me to get food. When we made it back we all sat down and ate and laughed at uncle C. He would drink but he was funny he thought that he was Prince. After he finished eating he put his headphones back on and sung Prince and Michael Jackson songs all night. Uncle G kept getting up and screaming in the living room telling him to shut up and he would for a while and then he was back at it. I went to bed later over in the morning. I laid there with my eyes open looking at the ceiling wondering what would happen. After hours of being afraid I finally fell asleep I slept peacefully all night over into the afternoon when I woke my uncles greeted me in a kind manner. Uncle G asked what I wanted to eat I told him and I took a shower. When I finish showering he prepared my meal and he said that he was going to take me shopping to get things that I needed and to try to get me enrolled in school. I went with what he said but in my head, I kept telling myself that it wouldn't last long because nobody was ever kind to me. I got dressed and ate and we left uncle C came with us. He was always talking mess and he loved the women everywhere we went he was flirting with one. Everything I asked for they bought me they even bought me things that I didn't ask for then we went to lunch and I met uncle G's girlfriend she was so sweet and so beautiful and she said that if I needed anything even if it was just to talk please call her. This is the nicest anyone had ever been to me and I still did not believe in them. We left the restaurant and went to the school my uncle talked to the lady in the front office he said that he had known her for 20 years. She pulled my records and then she told him that my records showed that I was in the seventh grade. He couldn't understand how my birthday was in February and I was 13 years old getting ready to be 14 in the seventh grade as he talked to her I stared into the distance. I did not care anything about school the few times that I was there I didn't learn much anyway are I was being made fun of. He turned and touched my arm and asked me if I had failed a grade or 2 and I just told him that I didn't know. He enrolled me and we left. in the car he asked me again how this had happened he said did you get held back and I told him no I just never was really allowed to go to school it was not important in our house. A look of shock came on his face and his eyes filled with tears and he didn't say another word. When we made it home uncle G cooked dinner while I sat on the front steps enjoying the breeze that blew through my nappy hair and the sunlight that embraced my face while the tears creeped from my eyes. All I could think about was my brothers and sisters and the hell that they were going through and that I had no way to make it better. The sun slowly left the sky and it started to get dark. My uncle asked me to come in and take my shower and that I did. After I showered we sat down at the table and he asked if I could bless the food I told him (No). He asked why? I said that I didn't want to he said didn't your mother make you bless your food or give thanks to God before you ate? I paused then said we hardly ate and there is no God. He said I'm sorry about that and that you feel this way he said God is real close your eyes and bow your head. He began to thank God for the food that we were about to receive, and he even thanked him for me and then he said Amen and we ate. After dinner I washed the dishes. Uncle G asked me if I wanted to talk about my life I told him no I didn't care to talk about it he said whenever you're ready. He asked me to lay my clothes out for the next day so that he could iron them for me for school. I was not used to this I had always done everything. I picked out what I wanted to wear and he ironed my clothes as we talked he said I have a few rules. you must go to school, you must clean up behind yourself because you're a lady, you must be respectful always say yes Sir and yes ma'am to all adults he said even if you don't like what an adult is saying hold your tongue and I'll handle it. He said you must come home after school and do your homework and get out your school clothes for the next day. He told me that my curfew was 8pm and that was all he asked. I was happy hearing his rules he wasn't asking for much and I had never had a curfew are was I able to just hang out and do things that made me happy. When I left my mother's house I didn't know what the inside of Walmart looked like I had never been to a mall are to a clothing store are a Carnival a parade are even inside of a restaurant other than churches chicken are McDonald's. I had never been to a park other than the park in the hood on deuce 9. For the first time I thought I might be OK. I just didn't know how to just let go. I said yes Sir and went to bed he showered and went to bed also the next morning he took me to school and made sure I got settled in. As he left he told me to have a good day. The day went well then it was over. I walked home and Uncle C was sitting outside waiting on me. He laughed so hard when he saw me, he said what's up dirty. I said hey he asked how my day went. I told him that it was cool I went into the house to do my homework and he sat there on the steps with his friends drinking and enjoying the day. When I finished my homework I got my clothes out for the next day and asked if I could come outside. Uncle C said dog you are good you don't have to ask to come outside. He said come on out, he told me that he had someone that he wanted me to meet we walked up the block to this apartment building on Marcus and Natural Bridge he introduced me to his lady friend. She had five children me and her oldest daughter were about the same age and we became good friends over the years. My mother was an alcoholic and on drugs. My mother had abandoned me and her mother was on drugs she was the oldest of 5 children and she took care of her brothers and sisters on the days that her mother didn't. Her mom was still cool though and funny as hell she was nothing like my mother me and T started hanging out a lot we went to different schools but after school we chilled on the block at her house most of the time. My uncles were good to me I remember a week before my 14th birthday I came on my period I was terrified

I didn't know what to do, I sat there in me and my uncle G's room all day waiting for him to come home from work when he came home. I said to him I'm sorry but I'm having my period he asked why are you sorry? I told him that I didn't want him to be mad at me. He then hugged me so tight and laughed and said baby no it's a natural part of life. He said put your coat on and come with me. We went to the store and he bought me seven different things to use I did not even know that they made all of these different products and different sizes. After shopping we stopped for ice cream and went home. When we made it home Uncle G told me to go shower and he said he was going to call his lady friend, after my shower she was there and she came into the bathroom and picked out a box of pads and showed me how to use them. She then kissed me on the forehead and said you are ok! Everything is alright she held my hand and we walked out of the bathroom she had a card and a little cake congratulating me she said you are now a young woman. We all ate cake and watched TV and then went to bed. A whole year had gone by and I still had so much anger and pain inside of me even though my life was good for the first time I began to rebel hard. I started hanging with the wrong crowd and smoking weed. I was jumped into a neighborhood gang. I stopped going to school every day and started fighting all the time. I was heartless and getting into a lot of trouble. It didn't mean anything to me how great my uncles were I still felt empty, lost, broken and confused and I felt like smoking weed helped to kind of take the pain away and alter my thoughts. Uncle G didn't give up on me though. He told me that I would go to school even if he had to go with me and sit in class with me. It lasted for a little while but once he stopped coming so did I. I remember bringing my report card home and I had all Fs and my Uncle put it in a picture frame and put it on the wall. He showed everybody I guess he thought that the embarrassment would change me but it only made me hate school even more. I really didn't care about anything. Things became so bad that my uncle moved me from a city to a different school district and away from the people I called friends. That didn't make it any better we lived in the hood in Hills Dale around the corner from Pine Lawn and everybody at my school Normandy middle school was thugging. I was a blood and I fit right in. We lived near my uncle G's mother I called her grandma and she loved the ground I walked on. I could do no wrong in her eyes she called me Daisy she would safe driving miss Daisy. I'm not going to let you drive me crazy from day one she loved me and was always good to me. I just didn't know what love was or how to love. She was always smoothing things over with me at my uncle he kept saying if she don't stop the thing she's doing I'm going to take her back to her mother. I knew that no matter what I would never go back. One day I went to a lock in at the palace skating rink and lit a blunt as I walked through the crowd smoking it the police grabbed me and took me to the front office. They told me that they were putting me out and that I needed to call a parent. I called uncle G at 4 o'clock in the morning and he was very upset. He asked me where I had gotten the weed from but I wouldn't tell him because uncle C had given it to me. When we made it home uncle G told me that I was on punishment for a month and I said we'll see and he slapped what seemed like fire from me. It didn't move me though. I went to my room and went to bed the next day we went to grandma's house. As soon as we made it upstairs I told her what had happened and she said to Uncle G you can't punish her 2 times for one thing she said you slapped her now that's good enough. She said I think that she has learned her lesson,

She just didn't know I didn't care one way are another I was going to do what I wanted to do. Uncle G said he would give me another chance but I better do better. A week went by and I ran into a classroom and beat a girl with the lock. I was expelled from the school district I left the school and went to one of my friends houses in the hood. I knew that my curfew was 8 PM but I didn't come home until midnight when I got there my uncle was sitting in the chair in the living room with all of my things packed. He said little girl I love you but I can't live like this. He said in the morning I'm taking you to your mother. I told him that I didn't have a mother and I went to bed. I still had that I don't give a damn attitude. I had told myself I'm all I got, and I lived by that. I had lived with my uncle for 2 years and I really didn't care about anyone or anything. Many people told me that they loved me but love meant nothing to me. To be honest I really didn't care if I lived or died and at this point nothing scared me the streets taught me a lot. When morning came he put my things into his car and he took me back to the old ran down duplex that my mother and siblings lived in. He knocked on the door and I sat in the car and watched the prostitutes on the corner taking off their clothes and twerking their bodies and the drug dealers selling drugs to any car that came through there and stopped. I told myself that I didn't care what happen I wasn't staying at my mother's house and if I did I would kill my mother, Tommy, and Donny and the police would have a reason to come and lock me up. My mother answered the door and she said why are y'all here? My uncle replied I can't control her and I don't know what to do with her so I'm bringing her back to you. She said I don't want her and she can't live here she said these kids in my house are messed up enough my uncle asked her what did she want him to do with me?

She said you can leave her things here on the porch and take her to her aunt Ree house she said she would call her to let her know that I was coming and that he did and he turned and walked away as swiftly as he had come. I still didn't care I had friends, I knew people and I could make my own life.

Poem How

What do you do with a broken heart that's torn so bad it wants to die? How do you mend a heart that's so overwhelmed it refuses to cry? How do you teach your soul to love when life is just a lie? How do you move on when your body shuts down and dares not to try? How do you allow yourself to be at peace when rage is all you know? How do you move on to have a better life when your mind and heart won't let go? How do you ask the man above for hope and to answer your prayers when he's so far away and your mother is near and she doesn't care to pray? How do you bring yourself to believe that there is peace when you pray and day by day the little Joy that you have it slowly fades away? How do you look forward to a life that doesn't exist and when you have nothing but bad days how do you not allow yourself to be pissed? How do you allow yourself to trust a world that is so cold? The same breeze that freezes this world sadly freezes my heart and soul. How do you let go of someone that you care for so much? Although they refuse to embrace you are give you that motherly touch. How do you keep it together without falling apart and how do you live life without your mind, soul, are heart?

Chapter 6

My mother sold everything that my uncle had bought me my smart tv, typewriter, all of my new shoe's everything but some of my clothes. She brought the few things that were left to my aunts house. My mother told my aunt that I would live with her until I turned16 and when I turn 16 they would send me to job corp. My aunt agreed. I just set there thinking how stupid they were I lived with my aunt for 5 months. one day I asked if I could go visit my friends. She said yes and I took 2 outfits 2 pair of panties and never returned. My aunt and my mother called the police and they put a APB out for me. I was smart every house the police came to my friends hid me and said that they had not saw me. The police and my uncles searched for me for months and my uncles left messages saying that if they saw me anywhere, they would kick my ass and whoever that was with me. I wasn't scared at all. I was hanging with T the young lady I met through uncle C. She was my road dawg and we agreed that if anybody pulled up on us and tried to take me we would fight to the end. A whole year had pasted I had slept in abandoned buildings at friends houses that would let me stay for a little while. I slept on a park bench and on a porch for a weeks. I went days without food but it didn't matter I controlled my own life. One day T and I were walking and my uncle G pulled up on us all I could think was I didn't want to hurt him but I wasn't going back. Me and T looked at each other, as he got out of the taxicab. He was a driver he walked over to me and said how are you doing little girl? I told him that I was fine, he said you know that I love you right? He said I don't want to see anything happen to you. He said my door is always open if you need anything. He took a key off of his key ring and gave it to me and turned and got back into his cab and left. By this time he lived alone back in the city on Marcuse and Natural Bridge the same apartments that we use to live in just a different building. Uncle C had moved in with his girlfriend on the Southside. My anger would not let me take uncle G's help. I threw his key and we kept walking. We lived from place to place for a couple of months and then I went to see uncle C. He was so glad to see me. Uncle C told me and T to come and live with him and his girlfriend. We moved right in with no hesitation. Uncle C house was the spot we did what we wanted to do. We came and went as we pleased and UNK old lady came with a crew. It was 12 of us living in a 2 bedroom apartment we kicked it every day and I didn't want or need for anything because TT and <UNK> took care of me but most of all I hustled my ass off. I kept money by any means necessary, I met my best friend when I was 15 years old. I didn't where life was going to take us are how this story would unfold. He was 26 years old and so full of life. He was fun, exciting, silly as hell and most of all family was all he knew. To take care of his family to the streets he stayed true. From the first day that I met him I knew that he was a special person with a huge heart at 15 years old I had a crush on this man. I loved his sense of humor and his silly ass laugh. I admired his boldness and his strength. Everybody looked up to him. I loved that from day one he was on my team. He gave me the game and taught me much wisdom. I promise that I had never met a person in my whole entire life that had the intelligence or wit as this man. When I met this him I was a motherless child and living my life how I saw fit. With no guidance, and nobody could tell me a thing. I met big Smoke through my uncles girlfriend he was one of her nephews. When I first met big Smoke we played around for a while like I was his girlfriend. One day he took me and my friend T to his mom's house for dinner, funny thing was we were the same age as his niece and babysitter. This made them dislike us very much but I didn't care. We left his moms house late that night. Big smoke and his friend took me and T to the hotel we freaked out. We acted like grown women, but we knew we were not ready for all of that. I locked them out of the car when they went to pay for the room. When they returned they were pissed. They began to beg us to let them in. After about 10 minutes or so they went back into the hotel and got their money back for the room. They came back to the car and asked us to let them in. I let them in finally. They cursed us out and threatened to put us out of the car on Natural Bridge. I knew that they wouldn't because they would have had to explain it to Smoke's aunt and my uncle. They brought us home and Big Smoke laughed that silly laugh and said (Lil Des.) you are not on nothing. He told me that he and I were just going to be cool from now on. Because he was to mature for me. He said you gone always be my Potna and I laughed and agreed but I still admired and looked up to him. As time went on I voluntary had sex at 17 years old after that I was a all around wild child. I used to always say whatever's clever. I was always down for whatever if it didn't make money it didn't make sense. Smoke taught me the streets and I was blessed with the gift of gab and hustling was in my blood. I had to get it at any means necessary. Big smoke ended up dating my best friend T's mother. She was homeless so she came and lived with my uncle and his girlfriend too. Smoke had 2 kids with her but the relationship didn't last because smoke found out about her use of cocaine. His 2 children live with his mother and T's mother continued to live with us. Smoke and some of the other guys were kind of in and out of the house from time to time. They lived with their girlfriends or when things went bad they would come and spend a night at TT house or stay a couple of days, or even stay until they got a new chick. T started dating Big Smoke little brother Lil Daddy but she was sleeping around with a few of my lil friends and she taught us ain't no fun if the homies can't have none and that's just how it was. I really didn't care I dated a lot of men for the money. I loved the money but hated men. I played them every chance I got. I would tell them I loved them just so they could take care of me. I would have sex with three are four men a day sometimes more. I was addicted to sex and money, car's, clothes, and shoes made me feel complete. Because I had a pretty face And a fat ass that's all that men saw, when I saw them I saw dollar signs. I learned that men played games but they couldn't beat me. I told them everything that they wanted to hear and they ate it up. After I got my way are used them for all I could use them for I disappeared. Then I met this woman at my cousin job she was cool as hell but she was a lesbian. She used to come over to our house all the time and hang out. Then one day she started buying me things. Panties, clothes, and she knew I loved pooh bear she would buy me bears and jewelry. She always took us out to restaurants and to parties she was cool people. One day we came home from hanging out and she asked me for a kiss. I was shocked, I asked her what would that prove? She said just kiss me, I kissed her and it was amazing. After the kiss we talked for hours sitting on my cousins bedroom floor. I was 17 years old and she was 28 she wanted to date me and I told her I had never dated a woman before. She then said it doesn't matter I just want to be with you. She said we can take it as slow as you like so I agreed. She lived with a woman but she hardly ever went home to her. She was infatuated with me and I was turned on by the thought of having somebody so into me. Months went by and I still had a few boyfriends and I played around with my little girlfriend no strings attached. One night we had a few drinks and started to kiss. She kissed me on the neck as she caressed my breast. She slowly removed my shirt and pushed me onto the bed. She climbed on top of me and kissed me deeply. My entire body tingled! I knew that this wasn't right but I needed her and I was very curious to know how it would feel being touched by another woman. I knew that just from the thought of touching her or her touching me my vagina got wet and ran like a river. I had to see what she was about. She began to lick me all over my chest and then she gently sucked my small breasts. She had a Cup that she took pieces of ice from she rubbed ice from my neck down my chest to the center of my stomach. When she made it to my vagina she came up and whispered in my ear and asked Are you ready? I softly replied yes! She put the ice in her mouth and kissed and licked me like I had never been licked before. After she finished taking me on the ride of my life. She covered my body and we laid there and she said I don't want you to do anything to me until you're ready. She said we have all of the time in the world and she held me and we fell asleep. I was blown away this lady had not only touched my body but she had touched my mind. The next day we hung out all day when night came she said that she was going home to get a change of clothes. I told her since she was going to Illinois, I was going to ride with her so I could stop by my mother's house since it had been so long and I hadn't seen my siblings. We went by my mother's house and she actually opened the door and let us in. I greeted her with a smile and a hug. I introduced pat to her and I told her that she was my girlfriend. My mother called my sisters and brothers over to her side of the house to see me. I hugged and kissed them and let them know how much I had missed them. They really didn't say much they just looked at me. I could see sadness and sorrow all over their little faces and my baby sister would not let me touch her because my mother didn't take the time out to teach her that she had a big sister other than the ones who lived in the house with her. This broke my heart into pieces and tears filled my eyes. I took a deep breath and swallowed what felt like a horse pill in my throat I collected myself and continued my visit. My mother told my brothers and sisters that Pat was my little girlfriend and stood up and grabbed her hand and pulled her over to her and started slow dancing with her to the music that played on the radio. I walked over to the other side of the house with my siblings and my mother didn't say a word. She continued to dance while holding a colt 45 in one hand. While on the other side of the house I talked to my siblings. I was trying to see how they were doing or if they needed anything. My sister under the baby boy said to me why do you care? She said why are you here we don't like you because you think you are all that. She said go back where you came from. This destroyed me and I couldn't say a word. I turned and walked back to the other side of the house where Pat and my mother were. I told Pat that I was ready to go and she turned and said goodbye to my mother. My mother stood up from the bed walked over to Pat put her arm around her neck and kiss her in the mouth. When Pat stepped back my mother said you don't have to be scared with your fine ass. My mother and I began to argue and she kept trying to get in my face and fight over my girlfriend but Pat stood in front of me. As I walked to the door she talked to me like I was a stranger on the street she told me all about how she would beat my ass. I told her to try it! I told her that I was not a little girl anymore and that I would hurt her. She said Hoe keep talking I'll go get my gun and shoot you in your face. I told her that I wasn't moved at all. I said do what you have to do. By this time she stood on the front porch talking stupid while Pat and I got into the car. She told Pat that she could come back anytime and that she would suck her Pussy so good it would blow her mind. Pat never said a word I was so pissed. I told Pat to take me home. On the ride home I didn't say a word I just kept thinking how Pat had danced with my mother and let her touch all over her and never said a word and to top it all off the kiss. I told myself I was done with my mother and Pat. For some reason even though my mother treated me bad all the days of my life my heart wouldn't let me walk out of her life are stop loving her. Maybe it was because she was my mother or maybe I just had a heart of gold and was stupid as hell. When we made it to my uncles place it was a yard full of people. Pat parked and I told her to go home to her chick. I was done with her and I got out of the car, slammed the door and went into the house. That was the end of Pat and I and I was fine with it. Weeks later I started dating my Uncles girlfriend son. I really didn't like him much but everybody in the house was booed, up with each other so I wanted a live in boo too. He was much older than me and he had kids and he was one of the biggest hoes in St. louis. While we were dating he started sleeping with the girl down the street. She was a year younger than me. Now don't get me wrong I was a hot mess too. He wasn't going to outdo me (baby)! One day the man downstairs from us told me that he would give me $150 dollars to suck my vagina. Well I went for it I went into his apartment and he picked me up and sat me on the table in his kitchen and went to work. He kissed my inner thighs and moved his way up to my girl. I can't lie he knew what he was doing after 20 minutes it was over and I had my money. I came out of his apartment and Big Smoke, and his boys were sitting on the porch. We all laughed and smoke said man you are wild as hell. I didn't care what he said or how they felt. I bragged about it and I told them that since they cousin wanted to play. we could play! I said to them he's dating the girl down the street and she is bottom of the barrel. meaning (but ugly) Oh how we laughed until he got home. When he made it home Big Smoke, Li Daddy, and Mike told on my ass. They told him everything that I had said and done. Honey he was so mad, He cursed me out and slapped me so hard I fell and cut my back on a glass table. I got uo and said so what this wont make or break me. I told him that it was over. The next day I moved in with my cousin I was still out of control and I still hung out at my uncle C house all the time. That was where everybody played cards, domino's, shot dice, got drunk and high and talked all kind of mess. We had tons of fun. Unc's house was always full of people. One night I spent the night at my uncle house. T was at her baby daddy house. Yes! she was pregnant by a guy with my cousin. He lived in Illinois and when she wasn't with him and at home, she dated Lil Daddy so on this night everybody else was gone somewhere doing their own thing and me and my uncle girlfriend and Lil Daddy were at the house. Lil Daddy kept coming on to me, I told him that I was not interested because he dated my girl. He didn't care he kept telling me how he really liked me and she was just something to do. I didn't care what he said I was not going down that road with him. He kept pushing so I went and got in bed with his aunt. She was already sleep and he followed me and got in the bed beside me I asked him to go back into the living room but he refused. He said I just want to hold you at this point I didn't think he would do anything to me so I wasn't afraid. We laid there and he gently whispered as he talked to me and a little while later the both of us fell asleep and he just held me as he said he would. The next morning TT saw us in bed with her. She asked what we were doing and why we were in her bed and I told her I came in there and Lil Daddy followed me. She really didn't care she didn't get in anybody's business and Lil Daddy was her nephew. So she wasn't going to say nothing to anyone about anything. Lil Daddy told me that he was not going to give up until he got me. I laughed at him and told him to get over his self. I walked into my cousin room and he walked behind me and said look when I turned around. He had his penis out in his hand This fool was hung like a horse, I said Oh my God! So that's how you get women to sleep with you? He said yes it always works he said once I show them, I got them! I said sorry but that doesn't impress and I walked out of the room as the day went on T and Big Smoke and Mike had come to the house we laughed and played around and talked mess like nothing had happened. I really didn't take Lil Daddy serious. he was just trying to see if I would let him hit typical dude stuff. I knew how dudes were and I wasn't going to play that game with him. After that night I started coming over less and less I began to get caught up in life. While living with my cousin her and her husband were acting like asses and her husband couldn't keep his hands to himself so moved out. I had met this white girl that lived next door to my cousin. I moved in with her. Her name was Shay she had 3 boys and she was cool as a fan. She drank all the time and smoked weed and so did I and we connected immediately. I started stripping at this little spot in Illinois, I loved the fast money and it was easy. I still had my hustles and schemes on the side and I didn't care what anybody had to say. T and I had been friends for years and she started to throw shade and talk bad about me to her newfound friend the girl down the street that my ex was dating. Every time I turned around she was telling somebody I was a hoe, or a slut. When I came around she would act like we were so cool but I knew better I just played alone. It's funny how people will judge you and what you do and forget about their errors in life. Messy is what they are. Lil Daddy got an apartment on 39th and Shaw and everybody moved in with him except for my uncle and his aunt and their daughter. I even stayed for a little while. One night Lil daddy had a birthday party and we all were so drunk. After the party we all went home and climbed in bed with Lil daddy. Myself, T, and one of our other friends that night I raped Lil daddy but he was all in. My friends laid next to us in bed pasted out. While I took this man for a ride of his life and I was not bothered at all by what my friend would think. She had slept with plenty of my boyfriends and that didn't bother me either. I was just enjoying my night it just happen to be with her man on some silly shit. Lil daddy had been trying to have sex with me for years this night I just gave in. A few months later I found out I would soon be having his baby and this broke my spirit and sent my world crashing. My supposed to be friend turned her back on me after all of the dirt that she had done to me she had the nerve to be in her feelings. She walked away with ease. I learned that I was alone and my baby daddy could care less about me are my unborn child. I was a 18 year old drunken stripper that hustled my ass off in these streets yet I was still empty inside.

Poem I wish

I wished that you were there when I closed my eyes. I wish that you were there so I could say my final goodbyes. I really wished that you were there to hug and kiss me and say baby it's alright and to tuck me in and say I love you goodnight. I wished that you were there to see me fall in love for the first time so that when I got my heart broke you could have told me having my heart broke should be a crime. I wished that you were there for my 16th birthday. (hell) I even wonder what you would have had to say. I wished that you would have hugged and kissed me instead of every time I came around all you could do was dismiss me. I wished that things were better than they are but nothing has changed its still the same so far. I wished that wishes could come true. Maybe they don't maybe they do but I'll stop wishing because mine didn't not even a few.

Poem I am Sorry

I am so sorry my friend. I want you to know that I carry you deep within and I pray that one day our hearts will mend. I am sorry for so so many things. I also miss the glow in your eye and the joy that friendship brings. We were So young and made decision that we somehow regret. I just want you to know if I could turn back the hands of time. I would only ask for my friendship back. I was wild, I was dumb, I was irresponsible and now we have to deal with what we have done. I see things differently now things that when I was a young girl I didn't see. All I want now is for you to forgive me. I'm sorry for being such a smart ass and for acting like our friendship didn't mean much. You were my soul sister and my heart you deeply touched. I am sorry about all of this mess with this man but you said ain't no fun if the homies can't have none when we were just little girls. Who knew that he would come alone and destroy our world? You said that it didn't matter as long as we didn't love them. Who knew that I would love him and you would to? You never said nothing about kids but now they are here and we don't have a simple hello or goodbye for each other and for them that I fear. We are ex friends raising distant siblings you know. We are grown women now and enough time has passed I think that we should leave the past in the past and just let go. We are adults now and one day I pray that we act as though. I also kind of understand that you're in your feelings and that this was a low blow. I just want to say I'm sorry but truth is life goes on and wishes don't come true. So long my friend God bless you and your children boo.

Chapter 7

My grandmother used to call me and pray for me quite often and I would tell her there is no God. I would beg her not to talk to me about God or what he could do for me. I asked her how does a God sit high and look low and have all power in his hands and allow a child to be raped, beat, molested and homeless? She said no matter what child I am going to keep praying and standing in the gap for you. I didn't tell her that I was pregnant because she had already said enough. I just ended the call with a simple I love you. As the months passed I stopped stripping and the streets became all I knew and thanks to big Smoke he made sure that no matter what I was cool. He always had a street connect for me or a couple hundred dollars every time I saw him and vice versa. We made runs together, we took trips together, We hung out all the time his family was my family specially since my uncle was basically married to his aunt. I remember on our last trip to Phoenix Arizona big smoke said once we make it back home. I got something that I really need to talk to you about. At the last minute the business deal changed and smoke said I need you to handle this other business. I said whatever clever, instead of him driving back I did and he took my place on the greyhound. Me and the big homies made it back untouched but smoke got jammed up. He did not make it right back home. He was arrested in Oklahoma and they were trying to give him 20 years but money talk. A little time went by and I looked up to see his face and hear that silly laugh and life was great again. I had my best friend, my talk to buddy, my personal bodyguard and one of the coolest dopiest guys I had ever known back on the streets. Weeks later we finally had that talk. Big smoke said Des I'm in love with you. He said you are my ride or die chick and I have loved you for a long time. He said that he had wanted to ask me out for a long time but I had slept with Lil daddy. He also said that I had told him that I was carrying Lil daddy baby. He then went on to say that he had a talk with his little brother and that he had said that I was a hoe and that I was not pregnant by him. Lil daddy told his brother that he would not touch me with the dead man's dick. I wasn't upset when I heard this he had said it all before. Big smoke said I love you and I don't care who's baby it is. He said Des you're my right hand man, my dirty buddy and I know that you're not a hoe. He told me that he needed me in his life. I started laughing really hard and said I swear that this is your brother's baby! I told him that I could not miss with him because it was not right. Big Smoke said ok if I ask my brother if he's ok with me taking you on a date can I at least take you to the show? I said yes! A week later Lil daddy called me and cursed me out and told me to stop telling people that I was carrying his baby are that he had even slept with me. When I hung up the phone I told myself to hell with Lil daddy help yourself help you sister Debbie At the last 2 years big Smoke was locked up for 4 years I talked to him often and I knew that he was coming home soon. I told him Boo I got you I'm going to put you back in the game he knew about me and Will but it didn't bother him he knew that my loyalty was with him. The streets had been talking meaning everybody and they momma were running up to the jail house throwing dirt on my name. Lil Daddy and the rest of Smoke family had told him that me and Will lived together and that Will was strung out on heroin and I was using too. Little did they know that wasn't my life and Will was grown and did what he liked.

Poem Words

Is it true that words are so strong they can damage your soul? Bruise the toughest ribs and leave your heart with a hole? Touch you in places that you have never been touched and make you hurt over things that you miss so much. Words can leave you feeling empty inside and sometimes if a person says the wrong thing it has an effect on your pride. Is it true that words can change your whole way of life, your outlook on everything? Words can also make you forget what the word life really means. Words can feel your heart with joy and also cause you pain leave you feeling happy inside yet bring you much Shame.

Chapter 8

The day came and Smoke touchdown I remember hearing a knock at the door. My uncle G answered it I heard him saying what's up big smoke! I could hear them talking and laughing after a few minutes my uncle said Des. and Will are back there. My uncle knew that Smoke was my heart. Will and I were in bed watching tv. I was laying behind him when Smoke walked into the doorway and said what's up Will? Will said nothing much what's up with you Big Smoke? Smoke said s*** then he said what's up Lil Des! I said hey boo! Then he said this s*** here is over! Let's go Des.! I got up got dressed and told Will that I would be back and smoke and I left. I left my son with my aunt and uncle C and Smoke and I got a room. I was so happy to see him. To be able to touch him I remember us sitting in the jacuzzi and him holding me in his arms crying telling me how I meant the world to him and that he didn't want to live his life without me. I wiped his tears and assured him that I was not going anywhere and that he meant the world to me and I loved the ground that he walked on. We had a few drinks and talked and laughed and made passionate love over and over all night. The next day I gave him ten thousand dollars and a pack and I told him I got your back boy! He laughed and said my nigga! He just kept staring at me and he said you are my ride are die for real. We left the room and picked my son up and went to his mother's house his mother had custody of his 2 kids by T's mother. At this time my son was going on 5 years old and smoke to were 7 and the other one was turning 4 they loved me. We stayed there for the entire day and night just having family time. Smoke mother had a welcome home party for him and everybody was there Lil Daddy talked to and played with my son but we never said a word to each other everybody talked about how much my son looked just like Lil Daddy but other than that they knew not to say anything to me about the situation. We partied, laughed, ate good food and just enjoyed each other. After the family left Big Smoke and I stayed up all night discussing our dreams and goals for our life and future. The next morning smoke told me that he didn't want me going back on the Southside where Will and I lived but I told him I make all of my money over that way and that was my house and my uncle G lived there with us. I told him I could go when I liked. I could not let the streets go they were my bread and butter and I hated to be controlled. My son and I return home my uncle was glad to see me he told me that Will had moved out and that he was back with his ex I was happy for him. I was not moved or dismayed I didn't care at all. Oh I forgot to mention when I moved back from Minnesota I moved in with Smoke's mother for a few weeks and after that back to uncle C and TT's house. At this time they lived in dog town and they welcomed me and my son with open arms. 6 months in my mother showed up I was shocked I had not saw her are heard from her in years. She was so small I could see her bones she wasn't the woman that I remembered at this time she was homeless and living in her car with her new boyfriend and my siblings were in foster care. She acted really happy to see me and she was overjoyed when she met my son. He had never met her but he jumped right into her arms. She stayed and talked to us for hours and uncle C told her that she could move in with us. I was OK with that even though she had done all of the wrong in the world to me I still loved her and I realized that I didn't need her anymore but now she needed me and I felt sorry for her and I felt the need to help her. I learned that my mother had cut back on the drinking but she was now strung out on crack cocaine very bad. I didn't look down on her though because uncle C and uncle G had been smoking crack for years and they were some of the best people in the world. I just found it hard to trust her and to believe in her overtime my world became her world and we became close. I enjoyed having her around and she was good to my son. I told her that I didn't want her buying crack I would give it to her but she did it anyway because she said I wasn't giving her enough. One day my mother and uncle C stole drugs from me and told me that my son had eating them. I was freaking out at first but then I realize that they were lying I raised hell about it but what more could I do? We moved from downtown to the Southside and my mother and son shared a room at uncle C apartment because I move next door and we hustled out of our place. After uncle G told me about Will I walked out of our back door and up the sidewalk into uncle C apartment where my son lived with uncle C and Smoke aunt and my mom. My son loved it over there they had him spoiled and he ran the house. I knew that I could leave him when I was in the street and I knew that he was safe no matter what might happen to me I knew that he was cool. I left and I hustled all night on into the next morning before I went home. I stopped by my uncle C house to check on my son. my mother had a guy there that wanted to get some work from me. But he couldn't go to the bank until 9 am to get money. I gave him what he needed and said when the bank open we are going to get my money. He owed me $300 dollars. I was tired and wanted to go to my place so I told him that he was coming next door with me. My mother said no leave him here I'll make sure you get your money but I didn't trust her. I kept telling myself they were going to try to scam me and they had smoked my work and I wanted my money. I was going to hold him hostage until I got my money. I walked in the door and my phone ring it was my supposed to be cousin through one of my uncles and he knew the man so I told him about what went down and he said I'm on my way I'll take him to the bank and get your money and bring it back to you. I foolishly agreed because I trusted him and I had done business with him before. He came picked up the man and they left 3 hours later he called me with this story about how the man went to the bank and jumped out of the car and ran. I had taken the man cell phone and driver's license as collateral. I told him now I know where you live so don't play with my money. When I got off the phone with ol boy the man called me and said I gave your cousin your money and they put me out of the car. he said can I please come get my things? I told him that my cousin said that he jumped out of the car and ran and he said if you bring me my things I will show you I pulled the money out of my bank and the time. Before I could say another word someone knocked on the door. I hung up the phone and walked to the door it was my cousin and 2 other men. I open the door and told my cousin to come into my room he said I got $400 dollars can you hook me up? I said yes and I took the money and told him I'm not giving you nothing. I asked him how you gone try to play me and come and spend my money with me? He began to talk loud and I turned to get my gun but before I could get to it one of the other men walked into the room with his gun in hand and as I stood there my cousin and his boys robbed me and took everything I had but my life. When they ran out of the door I ran into my uncles room and grabbed his little 22 derringer from his drawer and ran behind them as I made it down the stairs and out of the door they were gone just like that. I ran into the house and called Big Smoke over and over but got no answer. I called Will and he came right over to uplift me and encourage me. He also told me that for the sake of my son I needed to walk away from the street. I sat there disheartened and confused with rage running through me that I could not control. I wanted to retaliate but as I sat there crying. I knew that he was right I just kept telling myself that the streets were all I knew. I went to bed and Will set at my side and when I woke up. He was gone I called Smoke again still no answer. I walked next door to my uncles C place and told them what had happened. I talked to my mother and she said I told you to leave him here but you didn't listen to me. All I could do was cry they took 3 guns $7000 and everything in my stash I didn't know what to do. I made a few calls and went back to bed at 3am the next morning Smoke showed up and I was pissed. I asked where he had been and what good did it do me to buy him a cell phone if he wasn't going to answer it when I called? He just laughed this silly smug phony laugh! I began to tell him about me getting robbed I told him that I had to call Will. I will never forget what he said to me. He said I'm sorry I messed up again he said I was at the hotel with this chick named Nina. He told me that he knew her from back in the day. He said that my mom brought her to a couple of my visits when I was in jail and that they had been talking ever since. He said she's cool people he went on to say that they didn't do anything and that he had slept on the floor because he couldn't bring his self to do anything that would hurt me. As I sat there in complete and utter silence I thought this is the same thing he did in Minnesota. I thought after all I had done for us after standing by his side and holding him down all of these years. After playing his homeboy for him. Years of loyalty and honesty and being the chick that he had molded me to be. I was so caught up in him and his way of living that I didn't even know who I was. I kept thinking you betrayed me! when I needed you most you let me down your ride a die for some nothing behind chick. I kept saying he gained nothing from her he didn't put us in a better position he broke us for some chick. I told myself I wanted nothing else to do with him. He had broken my trust and our bond everything that I was he made me all of the scheming, game playing and running he had taught me and at this point I realized it was all just another game but this time I felt like I had lost and when I say lost I mean lost big. I finally was able to speak and I said to him I'm done with you. I'm done with this mess and I wish you and ol girl well. I told him I want you to leave he kept trying to talk to me I told him to shut up and get out. He left and went back to his mother's house and in 2 weeks he was back in jail because he had violated his parole. He tried to reach out to me but I wasn't having it and at this point I had nothing to say to him. Smoke told my uncle that he needed money on his books because he didn't have a dime to his name because he had put the hood on. Talking about now his brothers work for him but when he went back to jail they ran off with his money and would not take his calls. I told myself and my uncle that is his problem not mine. My uncle had given me $300 to get back on my feet and I was doing my thang but I started moving different. I wanted out but I needed to take care of me and my son and my mother when she needed me. I had dropped out of school the end of my 7th grade year. I had no skills and really had not worked that often in my life all I knew how to do with hustle. It was a month before Christmas and I had already bought my son everything he needed he was cool. A week later I went to jail because I had a warrant out for my arrest for not appearing in court for some tickets I got. I was in the County jail for 7 days when I got out I went home to find that my mother had stolen all of my sons Christmas stuff. When I said something about it to her. She got up in my face and cursed me out talking about she didn't take nothing but everything was gone. It was in my son's room under the Christmas tree he and my mother shared a room when I asked my uncle about it he said nobody had been in there but my mother. She started acting belligerent because she had been drinking and was high. She wanted to fight because I had told her that she was sad and pathetic and that it was real messed up that she would steal from her own grandson. She went on to say that I was a terrible mother and that I wasn't s*** .She wished death on me and my son she said that I thought I was better than everybody around me. She even had the nerve to say that I would never be half the woman that she was. In my hurt I stood toe to toe eye to eye with her and I told her I am more woman than you will ever be and I will never be anything like you. I told her you make me sick after all I do for you. You treat me like this and I walked into my aunts room looking for my son my uncle said that he had been at Lil Daddy house for a week with my aunt. I asked him why they would let my son go over there? He said Lil Daddy wanted to see him and he was not going to give me a hard time anymore. I was so p***** I called Lil daddy when he answered I asked him where is my son? He said how are you doing? He said I know that you don't like or deal with me but can I please get to know my son? Before I could say anything he said Des. I'm sorry for everything please don't keep him away from me any longer he said it's been 5 in a half year's please Des. I stood dazed holding the phone in shock I really didn't know what to say. Then I spoke I said I will see. My aunt came to the phone and told me that they would be home in the morning and that my son was sleeping she said that she would have him call me when he got up. I hung up the phone and hit the streets I had to replace all of my son's things nothing else mattered.

Poem

Lesson Learned

The Bible basically says praise no other God's other than thee but one day I met you and you became a God to me. I admired you praised and lifted you up (foolishly). Sometimes life has a you blind until that one thing opens your eyes and you can see. You realize that people have imperfections, lack of respect and they know nothing about loyalty. They have hidden agendas and plots and schemes and a unnatural lack of certainty. Yet they want you to keep your blinders on and pretend that one day they will be everything that you need. (Selfishly) Oh but one blessed day I must say I found the courage to walk away. I learned that no man is a God no matter how great he may be. I learned my lesson my eyes are open and now I can see. I thank God for this day because today I am free.

Chapter 9

The next day I return home. I have been thinking all night about a better life for me and my son. I was tired of what I was doing and I didn't want to be around my mother anymore. She was cruel and hateful and very toxic. No matter how good are kind I was to her she didn't like me and she was so disrespectful. I continued to do me though while figuring out my escape into a better life. Months went by and I had began to let my son visit with Lil daddy from time to time he was actually good with him . One day I came over to my uncles place and my mother had been sick she had a bad cough that she cannot get rid of. She finally went to the hospital at this point it was so bad that she could not breathe. When she got there they admitted her after running test they found out that she had tuberculosis and that she had it so long it had eating a tomato size hole in her lung she was dying and they were doing all they could do to save her life. They put her on quarantine but that didn't stop me. I came to see her every day I hugged and kissed her face I did anything she needed me to do for her. At this time I was dating this African man he paid my mother's hospital bills. I didn't realize how serious the whole tb thing was until the health Department got involved. They tested everyone that my mom had come into contact with we all tested negative for it but they put my son on medication to prevent him from getting it. I visited my mother in the hospital and she laid there unaware of what was going on around her. She kept calling out for my brother. Her favorite child he lived with my aunt in Mississippi . I called them and made them aware of what was going on but my brother never reached back out to me are her. He was living his life and didn't care about anything. As months went by my mother became stronger and the hospital discharged her. She came home and the health department came out and gave her medication to keep the T.B from being active. Weeks after my mother was home, she was sitting in the room on the floor talking on the phone to my grandmother. She had been drinking Colt 45 beer all day. I knew that she was drunk. I was in the kitchen cooking and I remember my son was running from room to room playing. My mother began to talk bad about me to my grandmother. She said that she hated me, and I was no good. I kept cooking and listening, but I was becoming so angry. How could she talk about me like this? I had been the only one there for her! I never talked bad about her without cause. I never treated her bad, but she was always acting ugly with me. I put the chicken in the greases, and I heard her say momma, she aint shit. I felt like I caught on fire I was so man . I stepped in the doorway and said "really, you aint shit" she jumped up off the floor, grabbed me by my hair and began to hit me. I fought back. She saw that she could not get the best of me, so she let go of me and ran into the kitchen and I followed her in there. She grabbed a knife and we began to wrestle over it. My son ran into the kitchen crying at this time, we were by the stove. All I could think was Lord please don't let this grease fall on my son and burn him. As we struggled over the knife blood was running down my arm and on the floor. I screamed for my uncle to come and get my son. I knew he wouldn't get involved because he was scared of my mom and they got hi together and he didn't want to mess that up. He came and removed him then finally the blade broke off the knife and feel on the floor. My mother walked off cursing me out. I washed the blood off me and I only had a few cuts on my hands. I was so mad I hit my aunts glass dinning room table with my fist, and it shattered. I turned the stove off and left. I hated living like this, I knew I had to get away. The next day my uncle called me to tell me that Big Smoke was sentenced to three years in prison and his mother was diagnosed with cervical cancer. He said that she was very ill and that the chemo was taking a toll on her and that she could not take care of Big Smoke kids or herself. I later found out that Lil daddy had moved in with her and he did all he could do for her and the kids but it was a big job. At this time my uncle house had been kicked in a few times and all of the old heads and old G; s around me were going to jail. I knew it was time for me to walk away from the streets before my son was left motherless. I had nowhere to go so I called Miss Maybell, Big Smokes mother and told her I needed somewhere to stay. She said Lil Daddy live here but you and my grand baby are more than welcome to came here. I waited two weeks before I moved in because I knew me and Lil Daddy were on bad terms due to the fact that I had been with his brother. He shocked me though he told Miss Maybell that it was ok for me and my son to move in and that he would be kind and respectful to me. I went ahead and moved in. I thought things would be weird and go really bad but Lil daddy and I got along very well. We took care of the kids and his mother. Some days she would be so sick that she could not even get out of bed. She could not eat and when she did, she could not keep it down. I would lay in bed with her and talk and pray with her and for her. I gave her babies all the love that she could not give them at the time. I made sure they had what they wanted and needed. I had a sugar daddy that gave me whatever I wanted, and I told him I had three children and he did for all of them when Christmas came, they didn't want for nothing, I made sure all of them were cool and happy. Four months of me living at Miss Maybell house Lil daddy and I would have heart to heart conversations about the past and our son and the relationship between me and his brother. One night while we were talking, he broke down crying and told me that it broke his heart to see his son calling his brother daddy and that his brother took his life. He said that he knew that he was wrong but he didn't want to hurt T, but trying to save her he realized that he hurt me. He said that he could not fix things with me or apologize because his brother had stepped in and was living life with his baby mama. He said that he had given his brother permission to date me and he was only acting hard like he didn't care but he really did. He said that he didn't think that things would last with big Smoke and I but they did. I set there with my heart full of sadness because I had never known that this man had felt this way. I did not know what to say I always thought and looked at Lil Daddy as a heartless man. He was all for self and didn't care how he treaded others he said I'm sorry Dee for all of this. Then he said I want you to know from the bottom of my heart that I have always loved and admired you and he said I always thought about you. He said you are one of the realest, prettiest, coolest, roughest chicks I know and you take damn good care of our son. He said I applaud you. After listening to all of this I was floored. This is a man that I felt hated me. He spit in my face before over some bull crap. He was always taking bad about me and now he loves me? wow! This might sound. crazy, but it all came to a full circle. I understood why he acted like he acted and felt like he felt. At this point I felt sorry as to before I don't care. I didn't think it was anything wrong with me dating his brother. I had told myself that his brother was just another man in the dating pool. He was not off limits because me and Lil daddy had never dated and Lil Daddy told the world that he had never slept with me and my son was not his. I told myself Big Smoke was fair game. Its so funny how when you are young you could care less about how someone feel about what you are doing in your life or about who you hurt but as the years pass you gain sympathy and understanding for others and try not to wrong or hurt people without cause. I saw my wrongs and I told Lil Daddy that I was sorry, and I never meant to cause him any pain. We sat there for hours smoking week and talking about life. I had a newfound respect for my son's father. I really never knew that this man was this hurt over the situation. All of these years he had just been playing hard. He really wanted a relationship with our son. Its true that clear communication is the key to everything. Lil daddy was good with our son and over time we became good. One day out of the blue he said that he really cared from me but he couldn't admit it before because people would judge him. He said that you were with Big Smoke and I was with T but at this point its just water under the bridge. Me and his mom just looked at him and he walked away. We clicked over time and I found myself caring for this man. He was sweet to me. He used to cook for me, run my bath water and he was always considerate when it came to me and my baby. One night after we put the kids to bed he said lets go have sex in the rain. I was caught off guard and scared, but I smiled and went. I needed this and I'm sure he did to. We went outside and he laid a blanket in the wet grass in the back yard. He began to kiss lips and forehead and then my neck. As he took off my shirt, we laid on the wet blanket and he removed my panties and pants. I was thinking oh my God am I doing this? He touched me so passionately he kept touching my face and looking me in my eyes and kissing me over and over and then he whispered in my ear and said can I taste you? Before I could respond this man had his mouth on me and all I could do was lay there and enjoy the moment as the rain gently sprinkled on my face. He came up and kissed me and slide inside of me. My body tingled all over he was the perfect fit and his warmth embraced my entire body. As he made love to me tears rolled out the side of my eyes. This was the best sex I had ever had in my life. He kept rubbing his nose on mine and rubbing my hair. All I kept thinking was, what is this man doing to me? After about four positions and three orgasm my mind was blown. No man that I had ever had sex with could beat him not even Smoke. When we finished, I just laid there. He took my hand helped me up and put the wet blanket around me and walked me in the house. I showered and got dressed and he did the same. We put the food away cleaned the kitchen, laughed and played around as if nothing even happened. As the days went by we became closer and closer. It went from nobody knowing to everybody knowing and we did not care. I had always had a hidden love for Lil Daddy he just pushed me into the arms of my best friend his brother. As time passed Miss Maybelle became stronger and she told us that she found another house and we needed to get ready to move out because the landlord wouldn't fix anything. We packed up everything and a week late we had moved. Things were going good for a little while but as Miss Maybell got better Lil Daddy started showing his true colors again. Talking ugly and acting ugly. Then his mother brother passed away, they were hurt but they handled it well. Miss Maybell gave Lil Daddy his uncles car and he started going out more and really didn't come home to check on his mother anymore. He felt that she didn't need him as much anymore and he seemed not to care about our relationship anymore. He began to show how cruel he could be. Once I saw that his mother was well I realized that it was time for me to move on. A week later I moved out into my own place. Lil Daddy and I still messed around for a while but he became abusive and he was cheating all the time. When I decided I was moving on with my life and I wanted nothing to do with him he wanted nothing t do with our son. I continued on with my life but my heart was torn. I was in love with one brother and infatuated with the other brother. Big smoke came home this time for about six months. When he touched down he showed up at my house and just like always he was happy to see me. We talked for hours about life and my relationship with his brother. He said that he was sad about the fact that his brother used to fight me. He always told me Des you know you deserve better than that . He said no matter what we go through I only what what's best for you and my son. I told him that it was cool and we were fine just getting along in life. I told him I was finding myself trying to figure my life out. His silly self-laughed and waked out of the door. He said I'll holler at you dirty and as quickly as he came he left but he returned every day to check on us. He always brought me and my son gifts. I told him that he didn't need to but he said you deserved the world but that I can't give you but I sure as hell would try. He would come over and bring the whole crew at times and we would kick it all night playing cards and bones, laughing and drinking till morning came and some days he would just come over and chill and talk mess about why we could not be together. Even though I told him that our time had passed, and things could never be as they were. He said I will never let you go Des. He said that I taught him how to love and that I was everything he had ever wanted in a woman. I told him to keep his game and charm to his self he laughed but never gave up. I continued to work on me. I worked on getting back in school and getting a job for what felt like the first time in my life. I had to be great for my son. For the first time I became so caught up in my own life. That I didn't have time for what was going on with anyone else. Smoke went back to the jail and we remained friends. this time he was gone for 11 years so much transpired in that time. I moved a way to Colorado for a year that's where I meet my soon to be second son father that year I became so home sick and after I found out was pregnant I moved back to the STL baby! I had an apartment, job and car when I came home. I was five months pregnant and my life was ok. My sisters had grown up and became woman and we began to visit each other and to learn one another. I was elated to see the wonderful woman they had become. When I move back I ran into Lil Daddy at my uncle's house he was living with them. When he saw me he acted like he missed and loved me so much. I fell for it I really cared for this dude and like a fool I was back in a relationship with him. A month before giving birth my landlord and I had a fall out and he told me I had to move out immediately. I was upset but I had sub leased the place and the young lady had not informed the landlord. I called Lil Daddy and he came and helped me move my things and I moved in with my uncle and aunt Lil Daddy, Mike, until I gave birth. months pasted and I gave birth to a healthy baby boy. He brought even more joy to my life. It seemed like everything was coming together. I had my siblings back in my life and my mother was coming around showing that she wanted to be a part of our lives and my career was coming together. The only problem word Lil Daddy he would not keep a job he was always fake hustling and a week after I had my son he jumped on me drug me from the living room through the kitchen and threw me outside in the rain and mud put all of my things in my baby things out. I had been working 2 jobs when I was pregnant and giving him one paycheck from one job and me keeping the other. most of the time he would blow his money drinking and smoking weed are trying to dress like one of the Joneses and he stayed in the club. I was a real fool for this man I bought him a car I did any and everything he asked me to and when we separated I felt like I was 2 inches tall but I learned from that situation and I have never been down there road again. pain makes the heart toughen it can't break. life makes you it only breaks you if you allow it to. When I walked away from him everything in my life was ok. I established a closer relationship with God. I set back and looked over my life and I realized God had his hand on my life all my life and I didn't even know it. I could have been dead and could have been in prison with the rest of them. I could have been and alcoholic drug addicted stripper for the rest of my life, but God stood with me and embraced me and my heart and saved my life. I am so grateful. Months passed and life continued to flourish my second sons father moved to IL with me. We decided to try and build a life together. I became pregnant with my third son and before I gave birth, he proposed to me. I was happy I felt that he was everything I could ever asked for in a man so I said yes. Things were cool for a while then I gave birth to my son and I found out my fiancé had been entertaining other woman. I was so hurt I became very violent. I went to his job to fight the girl and they called the police on me. I was told by the officer not to come back on the property or I would be arrested I had lost my mind. One night I picked him up from work and he got into the car and said something to me about one of the girls he worked with. I pushed his head and told him not to talk to me about them.

He pushed my head back and I saw black. I let go of the steering wheel and started fighting him. I had completely flipped out and forgot I was driving. When I came to my senses I could hear him screaming my name over and over for me to get off of him. I leaned over and grabbed the steering wheel we were going off the road. I jerked the wheel quickly. As I drove the rest of the way home I told him, that's ok you want to fight wait until we get home. In my mind I had told myself I was going to kill him. When we pulled up into the driveway he hopped out of the car before it came to a complete stop. And ran into the house. I parked and walked in behind him. He was nowhere in sight. I went into the kitchen and got a knife and went looking for him. I walked up the stairs to our bed room and it was dark in there. Just the light from the tv lit up the room. When I entered the door way I could see that he had taken his clothes off and jumped into bed. That meant that he didn't want to fight so I left the room and let the situation die. I was still so mad though. I called my mother like always and told her what happened. She egged me on. She would always tell me how I should beat the hell out of him or how I should stab him and he would act like he had some sense. I listened like a fool and the fighting became worse, to the point that he went to pick up his check and came home with a U haul. To make things worse I had forwarded all of his calls from his phone to my phone his phone rang to my phone and I answered it. It was one of the girls from his job she said may I speak to Teddy? I put the phone on speaker phone and said telephone he refused to talk so I told the girl he didn't want to talk. She said is he still leaving you and moving to Indiana? I was infuriated because she knew more than I did he was always gossiping and telling our business to the chicks at his job. He was messy that's why I was always fighting him I was so mad I let him load all of his things onto the U haul. Then I grabbed 2 bottles of bleach and went out the back door as he went out the front. when I made it around he had went back into the house I got on the u haul and bleached everything he had when he asked me why I did it I jumped off the truck with a knife and chased him down the street and tried to stab him. He had the neighbors call the police on me the police came asked what happened I told them. They asked him if he had all of his things then made him leave. He moved his things out and left me and the boys and relocated to another state. I was sad and mad. He was the one who had caused the problem and now wanna run. My silly ass listened to my mother and ran my boy's father, my provider, and my future husband off. I should have known better though, she was always causing hell in our house, like the time she told him my sons wasn't his and he had me give him a DNA test. Or like how we invited her over for dinner and she would come over drunk and start a fight with me or everybody in the house. She was always so negative. When he moved out she said good im happy. I started to see my mother more and more for who she was. It as funny how even though that chapter ended in my life. I was ok. I picked up the pieces like nothing had happened and moved forward. I had three beautiful sons that needed me and under no circumstances would I let them down. Months had gone by and I had become a independent well rounded woman. I loved and loved hard and my babied are my life. I worked in the medical field as a CNA and a CMT my kids and I were good. I gave them the life I never had. I promised to love them with every breath in my body and every inch of me and that's what I did. At this time I was 28 years old and I had found my way. I also started a new relationship with whom I gave birth to a daughter. When I had her my life was complete. I thought I had found my husband but after three years in the relationship he showed his true colors. We fought like cats and dogs because he was very jealous hearted and always angry about something. We were together for five years and those five years were toxic. I finally found the strength to walk away. At this point I had three different baby daddies and four wonderful children. those men gave me the best thing they could have given me. my baby's thanks move along.

Poem Trying to overcome

I sit here in my heart saddened with the world. Wondering how am I an adult but still feel like a lost little girl? Feeling condemned like a house that doesn't exist anymore. Praying and begging the man above to lighten my load and soften my cry because I sound like a lion when I roar. In my mind I meditate day and night trying to come up with a plan just to overcome. All of the madness and rage and asking God to please sustain me so that I can raise my little ones. Sometimes I give up it's like I've lost my way, so I fall to my knees and began to pray. I say lord please help me down this road. I think I'm losing my mind long ago I lost control. I say Lord please help me to overcome. Show me your way and guide my heart. Lord you said that you are my father so why are things so hard? I cry harder and harder and my screams get louder. I say teach me your way lord for I am lost and don't know what to do. I don't have any real family or friends my only hope is in you. I scream and I say, speak to me now! I just need to overcome and then I hear a voice that say my child your battle has been won.

Poem Inner Child

My inner child is so very afraid, lost and very cold. The same breeze that freezes my inner child also freezes my soul. I feel that my inner child has been misled. I also feel like all of the knowledge that I should have been taught. I was taught foolishness instead. I feel that my inner child is searching for love and peace. I need to be loved and I also need for my life to be at peace. My inner child is tired of being lonely and she pray that one day she will be free. Free from all of the heart ache and pain. Free from the lying and cheating and people looking for someone to blame. My inner child will never lose faith and she will always look to heaven just to make It through the day. It's a lot of things that my inner child does not understand like, why do woman give birth to babies and when they are still babies, they let go of their hands? Why is it that the people that you love are the ones that are always making mistakes and causing you pain and heart break. My inner child do not understand how a father can walk out of his child's life and still call himself a man. The disfunction and the hurt caused should have never been part of the plan. People say they love but not willing to take a stand. My inner child is sad. Why? Because she has never been through anything good, she has always had to face everything bad.

Chapter 10

Today I received a call from a long-lost friend, Big Smoke. I was so overjoyed to hear from him. He said that my uncle gave him my number. He said I hope its ok for me to call you. I said yes! how are you? He said that he was doing well, and jail had saved his life. He expressed that he had learned so much that he wanted to share with me. He told me he had started writing poetry like me but he laughed and said I'm not cold at it like you but I'm cool. From that day on he called me all the time and I realized that the love that I once had for him still remained. He still cared for me. He was still his same old silly self but he had been through a lot of ups and downs just like myself. We talked for a year. We talked about life, love, hurt, pain. He apologized for all the wrong he had done to me and for hurting me. We shared stories of our past and present relationships. He informed me about all of the woman that had visited him and about the ones he had dated. He said that no one every mattered are meant much to him because his heart was always with me. He said that when he meditated the universe always brought him back to me. He said I was always dreaming about you or thinking about you. He stated that he really loved me. This was so hard for me to believe because he was such a lady's man. He loved all of the woman and they loved him. I loved him but refused to express it because he had hurt me so bad before. Even though I loved him as a person and for the man he was. I wasn't in love with him but I missed him dearly. He asked me to come and visit him and even though he was two hours away I agreed. A week later I went to go see him. When I saw him after all those years he still filled my heart with joy. We hugged and this mand picked me up and kissed me like a movie star. When he put me down. I was standing there trying to take a breath and collect myself. All of the inmates were clapping and whistling, and I didn't know that for years he had been telling them about me and how down I once was for him. He told them that I was the love of his life. I was out done and smiling from ear to ear while we talked. It was like he had never went away. For that hour we laughed and talked and realized that in all of my years of dating I had never known the happiness I had found with this man. He was so cool even though he was a hoe. No matter what I had done he encouraged me, he uplifted me, he schooled me, he never said a foul word about me and he always had faith in me. I couldn't understand it, he told me he had been studying religion and that he believed in the universe and that God was inside of us not in heaven. I told him I disagree. I said I believe in God. He said okay you can believe in your spooky God and I'll believe in what I believe in. He wanted me to read some literature on what he believed but I refused, and he laughed and said I see that your still the same strong headed strong hearted Des I've always known. Our visit ended and we said our goodbyes on the way home I smiled from ear to ear. It was really good to see my friend again and to have him back in my life. Over the years of him being in jail he got his GED and many trades. He studied business and began to work on a business proposal so that he can start his own business when he came home. In my eyes for a hood dude smoke always had his head on right. He just couldn't leave them streets alone I understood his way of thinking though he was a felon and any job he got was only going to pay him a little of nothing. He would always tell me that I got 15 kids. I got to get it how I live. When I made it home, he called me and he told me how I had not changed. How I was still so beautiful to him and how proud of me he was proud that I had overcome the struggle. Proud of the woman and mother I had become. I told him how proud of him I was as well I don't know why but we always just clicked for some reason. I continued to talk to him and visit him. I even took my 15-year-old son that he had once taken care of to see him. When we arrived they shook hands and shared stories about life and the past and plans for the future. As they talked smoke asked my son how he would feel if he asked me to marry him. I was shocked and could not say a word. My son said if my mom is happy I am happy! And the conversation continued on into a new subject. Our time had come to an end and like always I hated to leave him. On the ride home my son said mom uncle Smoke is a good dude. He said he always treated me like a son. He said he was more of a father to me than my own dad. My son looked at me and said it's cool if you two get married. I said son we have not talked about marrying each other it was just a question baby. He said okay but if y'all do it's cool and he slept the rest of the ride home and I was just in deep thought. I told myself that no matter what Smoke and I could never be and now that I was grown I knew better and no matter what, I didn't want to hurt my baby daddy even if it cost me my happiness with Smoke. I made it home and showered and went to bed. The next morning bright and early Smoke called me. He said that it was good seeing us. He told me that we had made his day. I told him that it made mine to and boom came the subject that I hoped wouldn't come up. He said Des can I ask you something? I said yes! He said I know that we both have been through a lot but what's up with me and you? I paused and then said what do you mean? He said Des I tried to let you go out of my heart and mind but the universe keeps putting you in my dreams. He said I dream of you often and in my dreams your always happy and I'm the one making you happy. He told me that when he came home, he wanted to spend the rest of his life with me. For me that was a low blow. He meant everything to me but I knew that it wasn't right to marry this man. I told him that he was my best friend and he meant so much to me but it would crush his little brother. I wasn't willing to cause that kind of pain again. He said that his brother didn't care and that he didn't care how his brother would feel. He explained that he had been gone for 10 years and not one visit from his brother. He said that when he called home his brother wouldn't even talk to him. He said no letters not even the simple how you doing or a are you dead are a live? He said I don't care what my family think as long as we are happy. I told him that's not right and I wouldn't be the one to come in between their family. His mom loved me and loved the idea of me being with little Daddy but hated the thought of me being with Smoke. I was good enough for one son but not the other one. I told him that I did not want to cause a problem. He said to hell with all of them I just want you, I said I don't know this would be hard for me let's just see where God and time will take us. I wanted to say yes, I would spend my life with him because regardless of anything I knew that this man loved me, but I wasn't willing to hurt someone else trying to hold onto my happiness. We continued to talk, and he made sure I knew that he was not given up seven months had gone by and this time we had been back in each other's lives and talking on the phone for a year. A month went by and we continued to get to know each other and share stories. I realized that this man knew me better than anyone in my life and I loved that I also loved the fact that we had history. Smoke called me one day and he asked me again if I would marry him, he said that he wanted me to come to the jail and marry him right then. I was weak for this man and loved the ground he walked on. I cannot bring myself to say no. So I said yes. I would marry him but not in jail. I told him that the world had changed, and I want him to come home and live his life. Just be free and if he still decided that he wanted to marry me after getting everything out of his system, the women and the streets then we would get married and he agreed. The next day Smoke called my uncle G and told him that we were getting married and everybody and their mama started calling me and asking me about it. I was pissed because most of these people never called me not even to check on me and my kids. So, I made a status on Facebook that said for all of you nosy people that care so much about my business, yes I am marrying Big Smoke. He is the love of my life. Stop calling me because I don't care about your opinion. Moments later Lil Daddy commented. He was very mad and he called me every name under the sun except for a child of God and many of his other family members were very upset. I did not care it was my life and I told them just that. The next day I waited to hear from Big Smoke the day came and went still no calls two weeks went by and still I had not heard from him. I began to think that something was wrong. I called the jail and they told me that he was in the hole. They said no calls no visits nothing but letters. I felt so bad for him and I missed our conversation. I wrote him a poem in hopes that it would make his day and lift his spirits.

Poem

Sunshine for my friend

Sunshine for a friend I know that you are feeling down so I am going to bring the sunshine in. My friend, next to Kin, the only man whom I can depend. Let your head be clear, your heart be at ease and may your spirit have peace. I understand that you are hurt but let my words be like the breeze. Allow our pain to make you better I pray that I can lift your spirits simply with this letter. Just know that through the rain the sun will shine again.

Sunshine for my friend

My friend, Mr. Man! Oh how I love to see you smile even if it's for a lifetime are just a little while! Do not allow our rude and cruel actions to make you become disheartened, stand tall hold your head up your journey is just getting started. Let my words flow like rays of sunshine allow them to brighten and lighten your day just keep telling yourself that very soon you'll be on your way. While your on this journey to peace and freedom I know that it seems so far away. Just don't let abandonment and betrayal walk in and knock you off your square because despite all of the bull crap there are still some that care. Continue to be confident on this walk that seemed to never end and close your eyes and tell yourself I have sunshine from my friend.

Chapter 11

Big Smoke received my letter and poem and he wrote me back about a week later. He said that he was doing all that he could do to stay out of trouble because he was on his way home but he had got caught up in some mess and was in the hole. He also said that his heart was heavy and spirit was long but after receiving my poem and letter he was in a better place. He said I told you that the universe sent you to me. He stated that my poem touched him and uplifted him from such a low. He told me that he needed that and he thanked me and told me how much he appreciated me and how good of a friend and person I was. He said no matter what might happen between us I will always love you and you will be special to me after this letter I didn't hear from him for three months. I still wrote but I knew that he was going through a lot and he was getting ready to come home and I was getting prepared to move away back to my hometown in Mississippi. As time went by I had moved and I began to settle into my new little life. One day I got a call from an unknown number. I answered and it and it was Smoke silly self. I was very happy to hear from him. We talked for 30 minutes about him being home and me moving away. He said that he lived in a city with his sister. He seemed to have his head on straight. He said that he was looking for a job and a place so that he could get his kids from his mother. He also said that he was trying to start his own business he had so much talent. He joked around about us getting married. We both just laughed, and he said while I get my life on track you better not get a man down there in the sip because he won't love you like I do. I said boy shut up and live your best life. He then said that he was on his way to visit his kids. I told him to be safe and keep his head in the right place. He said all right dirty and our call ended. He went on with his life so did I. Everybody back home would call me to tell me how Smoke was still a hoe and about all of the women that he was sleeping with. I really didn't care because I knew that he loved women way more than he loved me. Plus God had blessed me to meet an amazing man a year earlier we were friends for a year. We talked on the phone day in day out. He became my best friend and me his. I began to really care for this man! It was crazy because I never really loved anyone openly. I loved Smoke because of who he was and because of our history but I knew that he was not my husband. I had never kissed this man, never touched him or never had sex with him. Yet he embraced my heart and he filled my emptiness. He was So humble, and different from me I was hard and cold when it came to letting someone in. I had been through a lot with men and in life I was just playing the field. Life made me, I didn't let it break me. He was kind and sweet and he would pray for me. He became my peace I loved Smoke but it was nothing like this. When I moved to Mississippi he and I started dating. I loved the person that he was. I loved the good and the godliness in him. I kept telling myself I really don't believe in love. I'm talking about heartfelt, heartwarming type of love. The fairytale love, the I will never hurt you in any kind of way love, the feel your heart beside itself type of love. I realized what

Smoke and I had was not real love or should I say it was not the love that would build us up. It was the time and memories that we held on to that we called love. I loved him but I wasn't in love with him and I held on because I thought what we had was great and forever that's because I never knew anything better and I didn't really know how to whole heartedly love a man. One day I told Ray that I didn't believe in love. I said love is not real it is a fairy tale. I told him that mothers love their children and families and you care about people enough to not want anything to happen to them but besides that love is just a four-letter word. He was shocked at the way I viewed things but from where I'm from it's all so real. He said wow! I'm going to show you that love really does exist and it last forever. A month had gone by and I had slowly began to Find My Way in Mississippi. On 2018, I received a phone call from uncle C. He said Des Big Smoke was in a car accident and he broke his neck. I dropped the phone. I could not believe it. My heart was so heavy. I cried my heart out. I didn't understand. He had been in jail for 11 years and home for a month and this had happened. I was told that things were looking very bad. I knew that I had to go home. I needed to see him. I needed to talk to him and most of all I needed to pray for him and with him. I needed to let him know that God is bigger than the universe and bigger than his situation. I needed him to trust God. That night I went to work at 10 PM until 6 AM when I got off I went home got my kids and got on the highway. I drove seven hours straight home. I took my kids to my family and drove two more hours to Columbia Missouri. When I arrived sadness was all over me. This is my road dog and my friends since I was 14 years old. I needed him to be okay. I needed him to live. I loved him to death he was a wonderful person and the closest thing I had to real family other than my uncles. I had my family but they really didn't know me he truly knew me. I walked into the hospital so scared. I made it into his room and he laid there swollen and sedate unable to talk to me. I spoke with his nurse and they filled me in on what was going on I held his hand and just cried. I leaned over him and whispered in his ear. I told him that I was here for him and that I needed him to trust God and I said I know that you believe in the universe but I want you to know that God is bigger and he will bring you through this. I cried so hard I kept telling him I need you to believe I need you while you're laying here to call out to God and to trust him. I began to pray out loud and the nurse in the room began to cry and walked out. I prayed until a calm came over me and the nurses came in to try and wake him. One of the nurses told me that he would never walk again. He would never talk again, and that he would never breathe on his own again. She said that he would be paralyzed from his chest down for the rest of his life. Hearing these words did not move me. I told her that God had the last say. I really believed that God would bring Smoke through this if only he believed and trusted him. I sat there rubbing his hair as he laid there on a ventilator. He had all of these tubes everywhere. I visited with him for two todays and drove back to Mississippi broken. I didn't know what to do. I kept telling myself that he needed me. I told myself that I needed to come back home to be with him and there for him. I didn't know how I would move back. I worked my butt off to get to Mississippi to make a better life for me and my kids and I had no money. I was living check to check working doubles just to make it weeks had gone by and I called the hospital every morning. When I got off work to see how he was doing. One day I called, and the nurse told me that they had taken him off of the ventilator because he was breathing on his own but he had a very bad sore on his bottom and a blood clot in his lung. A week later they took the trach out and he was talking on his own his sister had brought him a tablet and set up Skype on it so that he could talk to family and friends. I called him several times and he was always glad to hear from me but he was so sad. He kept saying this ain't living and I would tell him you are so blessed. You are still alive and everything they said you wouldn't do your doing it. I would tell him you have to see the good in this and he would say "I don't want to live like this. I told him that God would heal him and all he had to do was ask him to do it and believe that he would do it. He believed what he believed, and he was angry because we didn't talk all the time but I was so busy working and when I was home I was sleeping. He asked me a few times if he could come to Mississippi with me and me take care of him. I told him that it was too much of a job to take on. I said Smoke you have to get therapy and that sore on your bottom that's infected has to heal. I loved this man he was family, but my hands were tied, and it wasn't much that I could do I just kept telling myself that he's going to get better and he'll understand. We started to have fallouts because he said that he would call me and get no answer, or I wasn't calling him enough. I was working in the nursing home from 3 PM to 7 AM the next day. I could not talk on Skype or I would have gotten fired. When I got off he would be sleep and when he got up and called me I would be sleep I was doing all I could do to get the money to move back. In the meanwhile he became frustrated with me and told me his "best friend" that he didn't have time to play with me and that basically he didn't care if I called him or not he told his sister to tell me that I didn't have to worry about him and he asked that I not call him anymore because with or without me he would be cool. This really hurt my feelings because he had only called me once since he had been out of jail and everybody made it their business to let me know that he was no good and had not changed at all. He was living his best life and didn't give a damn about me but now he wanted to play the victim. Like I was abandoning him. I was really messed up behind this. My mind got the best of me and my heart sank. This year had been really tough for me. The end of last year my mother found out she had cancer. Even though she has always treated me bad I stayed by her side. I paid what bills she needed me to pay and my own. I went to every doctor's appointment. I was there through and stayed after surgery. I was at her house catering to her more than I was at my own house. When she became well, she started drinking again. One day I finally had the courage to ask her how could you do all of the things that you did to me as a child? She said what are you talking about and I ran everything that happened down to her and she said I thought you wanted it. I thought you liked it. I sat there full of rage and thought I would never do this to My kids. I told her how pathetic she was and I left her house. Some weeks later she called my daughter's father and told him that my daughter was not his and he asked me for a DNA test. I told him that I didn't have time for the mess with him and my mother. I said fine you can have DNA test. He called me the next day and apologized and said that he knew my daughter was his and he didn't want a DNA test. This was not the first time my mother had done this. Years before she told my two youngest boy's father the same thing and he requested a DNA test. I didn't care I knew that he was their fathers and the DNA test proved it. I figured out that my mother was a earth disturber and that she was very envious of me. She tried to break me so many times but I stood strong. It's really true when they say you live learn and grow. The hardest part about all of this is simply just letting go. Before I moved to Mississippi my mother was drunk and said to me I didn't ask you to do nothing for me when I was sick. You did it because you wanted to. She said you still ain't shit. She said that she never needed me a sorrow weighed on my heart heavy like never before I never opened my mouth and said a word. I just got up from the couch and walked out of the door. I cried to God and said you said honor thy mother. what do you do when your mother doesn't honor you are when she hates you for no reason? I loved my mother not for who she was or who she had ever been to me but simply because she is my mother. I left Illinois and started a new life in Mississippi. I tried to let go of all of the pain and hurt sorrow and the rage and madness but this thing with Smoke triggered something. I told myself from that point on after he said those words to me that I would not let him treat or talk to me that way ever again. I began to learn that it is okay to love people from a distance no calls, no visits, just live your life without them. I told myself that when he gets better and he's done recovering he would call me or I would see him around the way like always and we would be okay like we always were. I refused to stress or beef with him. I blocked him on Skype and Facebook, and I told myself that he would get his mind right this was in June. July 5, 2018, I woke up to a missed call from Florida. I called the number back and it was smoke sister. She said Des he is gone. She said he died this morning. I lost it! My body went limp. My heart shattered into pieces. I was broken I could not bring myself to believe it. He was doing so good. I just knew with everything in me that he was going to live and recover from this. I believed that this was just a test and that God was going to pull him through. I cried for days. I was so mad at myself because no matter what I should have been there for him. He was my friend and I let him down over foolishness and I broke our bond. This is a hard pill to swallow and there are not any words that can fix it. For months I was in a bad place. I could not believe that I didn't get to say goodbye or here him laugh that silly laugh one last time and it broke me even more knowing that he died alone. Its so crazy this situation had me broken but not only was I hurt that my best friend was gone. I was broken and really hurt because my sons father lost his brother. No words could express the pain. I wanted to reach out but I felt empty. I didn't even have the words. Sadness. Consumed me I was in a state of disbelief and I completely went numb. I was so hurt and after carrying this thing for seven I took it to God. I prayed about it, I cried out to God and I told him that I felt cheated. I told him that I needed more time. I had so many things to say to Smoke. That night I cried myself to sleep and Smoke came to me in a dream and he said what's up dirty? He told me that he was ok and that all he wanted for me was me to be happy. He hugged me and said its's ok. when I woke the next morning, I had peace all over me. days later God spoke to my spirit. I heard him so clear. He told me that I couldn't keep carrying the weight of the world he said you can't control everything. I heard just because you pray for something for someone doesn't mean that they are praying the same thing. No matter how you try he said you have to work on you and stop trying to fix everything for everybody. I heard peace be still over and over. Today I know that no matter what you go through. God is right there. No matter how low you are God changes things. Hurt will come and you may feel pain throughout this lifetime but always remember no matter how hard or heavy things may get. Call on God, hold on to his word because I know for a fact that sorrow doesn't last forever. Sometimes life will take you down through there, but I tell myself all the time, God had to take me through something to get me somewhere. So, I appreciate everything. My hurts and pains made me stronger. My weakest moment and downfalls taught me how to stand with grace and a smile when I felt like I was at my lowest and like I did not want to go on. I learned that I had the power and the strength to get up. No matter how much I felt the need to die. I saw that God continued to bless me to live on. Many people would ask me all the time if I had to do it all over again or if I could have changed my life what would I have done different? I tell them all the time, I would not change anything! Everything that I've seen and been through made me the strong woman that I am today. I am grateful I am appreciative, I am strong and I love myself and my children. I love life. It took a lot of work and a lot of time and so much out of me. So much working on myself to find my way and to figure things out. So many tears cried. Yet today I stand and I have peace and peace of mind. I have joy down in my soul that is uncontrollable. I love everybody. God gave me a heart of gold and even though my mother treated me the way she did and do, I pray for her and I love the ground that that lady walks on. I just know for sure that sometimes it's better to love people from a distance. I tell myself life is not easy but is sure could be a lot worse. I hear people say all the time, I would never do this, or I would never do that and I tell them never say never because you know where you been in life, but you don't know where you're going in life. Life sometimes throw you all kinds of curveballs and mentally you find yourself lost and doing some of the same things you never thought you would do. My life has been a real-life journey y'all and I'm still here. Most times we think that the enemy is fighting us because we go through so much in our life, but I learned that it is not always the enemy. God will put you in a situation to mold you and to push you to your greatness to shape you. You will just have to hold on and never give up. I had a talk with God one day and I said, God when I was a baby, I was told that there was a calling on my life and that you would use me! I said God I am getting old and I'm still waiting. I laughed and said what are you going to do wait until I'm an old lady then I won't be able to do much. Days later God spoke to me and said I've been trying to use you! God said "I told you years ago to write a book telling your story, but you didn't want to offend anybody"! He said but your testimony may save many. I was shocked and at that moment, I understood sometimes the things we go through may be a blessing for someone else's.

Poem Missing you

I tried to call you today, and as I sat there listening to the phone ring, I remembered that you flew away, Like the clouds at the end of the day. I sit and think. I never thought that you would take wings and fly so high beyond the sky, never to return or to explain why. Every time I think about you it kills me a little bit inside, Unsaid words, foolishness and holding on to pride and most of all because I never got to say goodbye! So many things unsaid, unable to clear my head, thinking about our last words. I still can't cope with the fact that you are dead! You were my friend, my next to Kin, my inspiration and to know that you are gone it breaks me deep within. I guess I'll have to pray that one day we will meet again.

My Story

This is my story don't nobody act berserk. I gotta face the hurt, express my inner pains, and open up and share the dirt. Through the ups and downs. I finally know that my lives not cursed and it's them bad days that makes me know what my life is worth. I was at my lowest point and realized I had to overcome and convert and now I'm standing tall flexing with my shame on shirts. I'm telling my story because I finally see the light of day and I'm thanking God for answering every single prayer, I prayed and the ones I didn't when I gave up and lost my way. I hope my story can help elevate someone to a better place and reminds them that no matter how hard you fall or how hard life gets just get up everything gone be OK.

To be continued.........

Words of encouragement

Sometimes the hardest things in life can be the best things in life. You have to do what's best for you stop holding on to the guilt of how walking out of a person's life would make them feel. Because if they valued your relationships' they would not put you in a position where you have to make that decision. We have to learn that our peace of mind and our joy and happiness are the key to life and the more we hold on to sadness and sorrow, hurt and pain trying to mend relationships that have obviously run their course. It only hinders us from reaching our true potential and the ability to have true happiness and understanding of what really matters in life. I have come to learn that old wounds heal but trying to forgive someone while they continue to throw fuel on the fire it only tears and breaks you down. It's better to forgive and let go are the ugliness in them will consume you. I have had my share of pain, I've been broken and rebuilt again and broken and rebuilt. Because I have tried to change people, I have tried to fix things in people that wasn't my job to fix. From the hurt and pain that I have received from those closest to me I had become sad on a daily. I was so hurt by their actions I almost lost me. Today I can finally say I am awake and my understanding changed and I realize that everything that I was going through I was only bringing it on myself. I loved hard I held on too tight, I wanted something for people that they didn't want for themselves. I cried about the dysfunctions that was going on in the relationships that I was trying to hold on to with others that was close to me. I prayed and begged God to fix and change things. One night as I laid in the driver seat of my car it hit me God can't change people if they don't want to be changed. He can't fix things if they don't see anything wrong with what they are doing. The more you overlook and try to forgive them and keep running back around or into their lives they feel like it's ok to continue to do the things that they do to you. Are say the things that they say to you without any remorse. The only way to fix this situation is to remove yourself and it's ok to love people from a distance its good for your health. I learned that sometimes you have to forget about others and take care of yourself. Because if you do not you'll lose you. I found myself losing me and cried out to God and he helped me regroup.

Printed in the United States
By Bookmasters